# SELECTED DOHAS

*of*

Kabir, Tulsidas, Rahim Khankhana,

Varind Kavi and Sheikh Farid

**Translated into English**
**and**
**Transcribed in the Roman Script**

— K. C. KANDA

By the same Author,

**Glimpses of *Urdu Poetry***

Published by

**Lotus Press**

# SELECTED DOHAS
## *of*

Kabir, Tulsidas, Rahim Khankhana,
Varind Kavi and Sheikh Farid

**Written in Hindi, translated into English,
and transliterated in the Roman Script**

K.C.Kanda

4263/3, Ansari Road,
Darya Ganj, New Delhi-110002

Lotus Press
4263/3, Ansari Road, Darya Ganj, New Delhi- 110002
Ph.: 32903912, 23280047, E-mail: lotus_press@sify.com
www.lotuspress.co.in



*SELECTED DOHAS*



ISBN: 81-8382-155-3



*Published by:* Lotus Press, New Delhi.
*Laser Typeset by:* Aruna Enterprises, Delhi-110 094.
*Printed at:* Anand Sons, Delhi.

# CONTENTS

# INTRODUCTION

The *Doha* (like the *Chaupai*) may be counted among the most popular meaures of Hindi poetry. It is a short meaure consisting of two rhyming lines each of which has, generally, a pause in the middle, breaking the couplet into four parts to enhance its musicality and rhythmic flow. The language used in a *doha* is by and large simple, straight-forward and speech-like; it makes no rigorous demands on the reader's powers of comprehension. The subject matter of a *doha* is generally ethical and edifying, of equal relevance to the commoners and connoisseurs alike. Because of its easy accessibility, and musicality, and the universal appeal of its thought content, the *doha* makes a quick impact on the mind of the reader and sinks effortlessly into his memory, so that he can relish its meaning and music at leisure. Apparently easy and short, the writing of a good *doha* is indeed a difficult task. It requires on the part of the poet a rich fund of knowledge and wisdom, a poetic sensibility, and a high degree of poetic competence to compress deep thoughts in just two lines of verse. Quite often, the poet also mentions his own name in the *doha*. As such the *doha* writing is, to use an old adage, the art of condensing a river into a pitcher. A good *doha* may be called a capsule of concentrated wisdom which, when unscrewed, floods the reader's mind with delight and enlightenment. It may be likened to an Urdu *shaer*, or to the Augustan couplets of Dyden and Pope, short and pithy, simple in style, but rich in content. "True wit," said Alexander Pope,

> True wit is nature to advantage dressed
> What oft was thought but ne'er so well-expressed.

The idea expressed in a *doha* may not be original, nor need it be embellished with tricks of fancy and imagination. Rooted in good sense, the *doha* should be morally and spiritually uplifting, and aesthetically pleasing.

The themes repeatedly treated by Kabir in his *dohas* are concerned with the moral and spiritual well-being of man, the soundness of his religious beliefs and practices, the propriety of his word, thought and action. Here are some of Kabir's famous *dohas* chosen at random from the selection that follows:

(*i*) I have nothing to call my own, all is yours, O Lord,
If I return what you gave, I incur no loss.

*Mera mujh mein kuchh nahin, jo kuchh hai so tera,*
*Tera tujhko saunpta, kya laage hai mora.*

(*ii*) Man dies but the lure of life and his lusts survive,
Eternal are our hopes and dreams, says Kabir, the wise.

*Maya mari na man mara, mar mar gaye shareer,*
*Asha trishna na mare, kah gaye daas Kabir.*

(*iii*) As fragrance lives inside the rose, God lives inside our heart,
Like the maddened musk deer, why seek Him thou in leaf and grass!

*Tera saain tujhi mein, pahupam mein baas,*
*Kasturi ka hiranjeon, phirphir dhoonde ghaas.*

(*iv*) In vain I looked for someone bad in the world outside,
But when I looked within, I found none as bad as I.

*Bura jo dekhan main chala, bura na milia koey,*
*Jo dil khoja apna, tau mujh se bura na koey.*

(*v*) I am bonded with the One who lives in one and all,
All are mine, I am theirs, otherness stands dissolved.

*Main laaga us ek se, ek bhaya sab maahin,*
*Sab mera, main saban ka, tinah doosra naahin.*

A few lines above I have pointed to the similarity of a *doha* with the Urdu couplet. A little reflection on the *dohas* cited above brings out the truth of this suggestion, for the main content of Kabir's *dohas* has also been treated by some famous urdu poets, and this underscores the universality of the ideas of Kabir which have also inspired different poets belonging to different climates and cultures. This also suggests that great creative minds, irrespective of their time and climate, think alike and return to the same fundamental issues of life and man in their writings. Cited below are five couplets of Urdu having a thought—content more or less parallel to the main themes of Kabir.

(i) Life was His trust, to Him it was returned,
In sooth I didn't redeem my trust.

*Jaan di, di hui usi ki thi,*
*Haq tau yeh hai ke haq ada na hua. (Ghalib)*

(*ii*) Thousands of desires, each a deadly force,
I had surfeit of them, yet I crave for more. (Ghalib)

*Hazaaron khwahishen aiseen ke har khwahish pe dam nikle,*
*Bahut nikle mere armaan lekin phir bhi kam nikle.*

(*iii*) He whom on earth and air I sought,
Was found to dwell in the den of my heart.

*Jinhen main dhoondata tha aasmaanon mein, zameenon mein,*
*Woh nikle mere zulmat khana-e-dil ke makeenon mein.*

(*iv*) Oblivious of our own faults, we found faults with others,
Once we saw the faults within, none else seemed depraved.

*Na thi haal kijab hamen apni khabar, rahe dekhte auron ke aib-o-hunar,*
*Pari apni buraeonpar jo nazar, tau nigah mein koi bura na raha.* *(Zafar)*

On all my six sides I find a vast mirror stretching wide,
No difference of saint or sinner now meets my eye.

*Baroo-e-shashjehat dar-e-aaeena baaz hai,*
*Yaan imtiaaz-e-naaqis-o-kaamil nahin raha.* *(Ghalib)*

If we compare the two couplets marked (v), one by Kabir, and the other by Ghalib, we are struck with the difference in style used by the two poets to convey the idea of unity in diversity and the presence of one divine Creator behind the cavalcade of life.

Kabir's *doha*, as it is meant for the common unlettered folk also, is couched in a simple, straight forward language, unadorned with imagery or metaphors. Ghalib makes use of Persianized diction and the imagery of a mirrored hall to suggest the oneness of God and His creation. Ghalib's couplet is meant for the connoisseur and the initiated reader who is conversant with the conventions of the ghazal, wheras Kabir's *doha* is accessible to every reader, including the man in the street. Ghalib's lines are surely more impressive poetically and are more richly expressive of the idea he is trying to communicate, but his verse is available to a comparatively small, elite set of readers.

As we turn from Kabir to Tulsi, we come across two main thematic strands in his poetry, pertaining broadly to the spiritual and the secular contexts. In the spiritual sphere Tulsi gives utmost importance to Ram Bhakti, which, of course, is understandable when we remember that he is the author of the famous Hindi epic: *Ram Charit Maanas*, besides being a firm devotee of Ram in his real life. Next to Ram Bhakti he lays emphasis, like Kabir, on the ideal of a noble life, based on good conduct and good sense. But we notice a difference in the language of these two poets. While Kabir's language is simple, natural and speech-like, some of Tulsi's *dohas* are couched in a comparatively sophisticated language. Tulsi was a learned poet and a master of both Hindi and Sanskrit. However, both Kabir and Tulsi are concerned with the moral and spiritual well-being of man, and are strong critics of the sham and superstitious in life and religion. Here are a few specimens of Tulsi's verse:

(*i*) Ram worship is a positive digit, all else is nought,
A digit multiplies to many, nought remains a nought.

*Ram Ram do ank hain, sab saadhan hai sun,*
*Ank gaye kuchh haath nahin, ank rahe das gun.*

(*ii*) Ram Bhakti is the gentle rain that blesses Tulsi's tree,
The twin letters, ra and ma, are rainy months indeed.

*Varsha ritu raghupati bhakti, Tulsi saali subaas,*
*Ram naam bar barn jag, sawan bhadon maas.*

(*iii*) Compassion is the soul of virtue, vanity is the evil's seed,
Abandon not compassion as long as you breathe.

*Daya dharam ka mool hai, paap mool abhiman,*
*Tulsi daya na chhoreye, jab lag ghat mein pran.*

(iv) The world consists, Tulsi, of diverse kinds of folk,
Greet hem all with a smile, it is a gathering in the boat.

*Tulsi is sansaar mein bhaant bhaant ke log,*
*Sab se hans mil boleye, nadi naav sanjog.*

The third poet included in this anthology, Rahim Khankhana, was not a saint like Kabir or Tulsi, but an aristocrat and a man of the world—a statesman, a soldier, and a scholar, yet a man of high mental and moral calibre. Linked with the court and the royal household of Akbar, he had a first hand knowedge of the grime and glamour associated with high places. His *dohas* breathe an air of practical wisdom, and a down-to-earth, "no-nonsense" approach to life:

Chop off the cucumber's head, rub it hard with salt,
This is the proper cure of folks bitter at heart.

*Khira sar se kaateye, maliat namak lagaye,*
*Rahim karwa mukhan ko chaaheye ihi sajaeye.*

This is the language of a hard-core realist who has tasted the bitter truths of life and has suggested a "tit-for-tat," remedy for such ailments. Or, read the following lines:

Snakes, steeds, guns and women, kings, men of lower breed,
Can recoil anytime, beware Rahiman, take heed!

*Urg, turang, naari, narpati, neechjaati, hathyaar,*
*Rahiman inhen sambhareye, paltat lage na baar*

Such *dohas* seem to have sprung from the poet's personal experience of intrigue and subterfuge associated with high places. Remember that Rahim's son was beheaded and his severed head was offered to him as a present of a water melon from the king. Such heartless cruelty could not but harden the heart of Rahim and elicit from him only bitter vituperation. But then there is sufficient thematic variety in the *dohas* of Rahim. If he talks of steeds, guns and kings, he can also indulge, Khayyam-like, in a romantic mood, and luxuriate in his imagination in the cosy lap of his beloved:

What use is paradise, or the wish-fulfilling tree,
Better lie beneath the tree beside your darling sweet,

*Kaah karoon baikunth le, kalip bariksh ki chhaan,*
*Rahiman, daakh suhavna, jo galpeetam baanh.*

Nor is there in Rahim a dearth of conventionnal ethics and morality:

Narrow is the lane of love, allowing only one to pass,
If "I" lives, God departs, when God arrives, "I" dissolves.

*Rahiman gali hai saankri, doojo na thahraaein,*
*Aapu rahe, tau har nahin, hari tau aapu naahin.*

Accursed are the folks, Rahim, who wield a begging bowl,
But worse are they who turn away a beggar from their door.

*Rahiman we nor mar chuke, je kahun maagatjaahin,*
*Ut te pahle wah gaye, jin bhook niksat naahin.*

Varind Kavi, the fourth poet in this anthology, also belongs, with Rahim Khankhana, to the category of the courtier poets, thoroughly familiar with the ways of the world and its rulers. In his capacity as an official poet and a pandit, he had served as a private tutor to rajas and princes, some of whom had mutually conflicting interests in politics and religion. He was for a short while attached to the court of Guru Gobind Singh, and had written laudatory verse in his honour. Surprisingly, he was also drawn to the court of Aurangzeb, who was, in matters of religion and politics, on the opposite pole of the Sikh Guru. And yet, Varind Kavi did not barter his self-respect and independence for the sake of selfish, material ends. He had the courage to criticize Aurangzeb for his fanatic zealotry, and his temple-breaking spree. But he was shrewd enough to avoid a complete breach of relations with the king. He had also served as a court poet with various other dignitaries, including Raja Jaswant Singh of Jodhpur, and Raja Raj Singh of Kishengarh. He had thus a first-hand knowledge of the goings on in high places, and his verses at times breathe an air of pragmatic, down-to-earth philosophy:

Self-interest is the force that motivates our lives,
The birds love a juicy plant, reject a tree sterile.

*Swarath ke sab hi sage, bin swarath kou naahin,*
*Sabhi panchhi sars tarn, nira bhaye, urjaaein.*

We should neither befriend the mean, nor antagonize,
Pernicious are his kisses, fatal is his bite.

*Hithu bole na neech ko, naahin bhalo ahet,*
*Chaat apawan tan kare, kaat swan dukh det.*

The fifth poet of this collection, Sheikh Farid, is senior chronologically to all other poets included in this anthology. He lived a life span of 93 years, from 1173 to 1266. He is more akin to Kabir and Tulsi, than to Rahim and Varind. Standing at the beginning of the book, he paves the way for the spiritual and ethical utterances of the poets of the Bhakti Kaal in Hindi poetry. His *dohas* and verse provide a rich fare of delight and instruction to the readers. Because of their easy accesibility, and deep ethical content, some of his verses have become popular quotations especially for the readers in the North. No wonder these verses have found a place of honour in the sacred scripture of the Sikhs, *Guru Granth Sahib*. Here are a few specimens:

*Be content with plain bread, and sips of water cool,*
*Do not feel tempted by the others' savoury foods*

*Rookhi sookhi hhaaey ke, thanda paani pi,*
*Dekh parai chopri, na tarsaeye ji.*

When someone hits you without a cause, do not seek revenge,
Kiss your enemy'e feet, Farida, pursue your noble end.

*Farida kuchh na kaho unhen, karen jo tum par waar,*
*Choomo unke paaon ko, pahuncho apne dwaar.*

Nibble away my skeleton, crow, eat the flesh from every part,
But pray, spare my eyes, with them I hope to see my Lord.

*Kagapinjar noch kar kha lo saara maas,*
*Mat chhoonayeh do nain, piya milan ki aas.*

The values of love, charity and fogiveness enshrined in these verses are of special relevance to the trouble-torn world of to-day, broken into the senseless divisions of class and creed, and overshadowed by the demon of religious fanaticism. If we keep in mind the lessons of love and peace, and of the unity of man and God underscored by nearly every writer in this anthology, we can perhaps stem the tide of bigotry and intolerance threatening to submerge and swallow this beautiful world of man.

I am grateful to Mr Zahid Abrol who has made a wonderful translation of the *dohas* and *shabads* of Farid from Punjabi in the Gurmukhi script into rhymed Urdu verse. This, in fact, has been the basis of my English translation of Farid. I hope the reader will find my effort aesthetically and thematically rewarding.

# Kabir
## (1456–1505)

# Kabir (1456-1505)

Kabir's life story is a mixture of fact and fiction. There is disagreement among scholars about the date of his birth, which is variously fixed in 1438, 1455, and 1497. Modern writers like Ram Chander Shukal and Paras Nath Tiwari, have however, accepted 1456 as the year of his birth. His parentage too is shrouded in mystery. He was born to a brahman widow, who, fearing public scandal, had abandoned the child near a water-tank, from where he was picked up by a weaver couple, Neeru and Neema by name. His place of birth, probably, was a small village three kilometres away from Benares. It is said that in his childhood he was fed in a mysterious manner by the youngling of a cow. They would place a pail beneath the udders of the cow, who, as soon as she saw the boy approach, would start spurting milk into his mouth. Kabir's parents trained him to be a weaver, but his strong spiritual zeal would not let him concentrate on the warp and woof. He was the disciple of Swami Ramanand, who was initially reluctant to have him in his fold. The legend has it that when one morning Ramanand came to the banks of the Ganges for his daily bath, he stumbled against the incumbent figure of Kabir, who lay waiting for the master. The Swami regretting his inadvertance, exclaimed: "Ram, Ram," and Kabir at once picked up the sacred word, "Ram", which henceforth became the guiding force of his life and philosophy. Kabir married a woman named Loi, who too, like Kabir, was an orphaned child, picked up by an ascetic vagrant from the river side. She was called "Loi," because she was found wrapped in a shawl, (*loi* in vernacular). Kabir had two children from this union: Kamal and Katmaali.

Another legend tells us that Kabir had incurred the wrath of the ruler of the day: Sikander Lodhi, who was provoked by the complaint that Kabir was an imposter pretending to be God. Kabir was tried and sentenced, to death. But to everyone's surprise, he couldn't be burnt by fire, nor drowned in river, nor crushed to death under the elephant's feet. He died, it is generally agreed, in 1505, though some people believe that he lived for 120 years. The manner of his funeral too has a touch of the supernatural about it. When both Hindus and Muslims were advancing their claims for his dead body, there came a voice from heavens: "Stop quarrelling, and remove the coffin from the face." Lo, the corpse had turned into a heap of flowers, which were equally divided between Hindus and Muslims, who disposed them of according to their respective rites.

We may not accept the authenticity of these stories, but we cannot miss the thread of symbolism running through them. Kabir's birth from the womb of a brahmin widow, and his upbringing in the house of a Muslim weaver, his wife Loi's birth and breading in similarly dubious circumstances, his dogged defiance of death at the hands of a tyrant, the transformation of the corpse into a heap of flowers — are all intended to expose the hollowness and hypocrisy of social and religious conventions, including marriage, caste restrictions, untouchability, religious divide and religious bigotry, to oppose which was the central task of Kabir's life and poetry.

Kabir was the leading light of the Bhakti movement which was aimed at protecting the Hindu religion from the twin dangers of internal weaknesses and the external threat of cultural and religious domination posed by the fast-expanding might of the Muslim settlers in India. The lamp of Bhakti lighted by Ramanuj in the South was brought to the North by Swami Ramanand, who handed it over to Kabir. Aided by the poetic and spiritual genius of Kabir this lamp made a signal contribution in dispelling the darkness of doubt and despair, and in bringing about a renaissance in religion and art. Consequently, Kabir's poetry has a pronounced didactic and ethical strain. It is meant, not so much to entertain, as to instruct and edify the readers. And as its aim is to reach the common man, it is couched in the language of everyday speech, which is basically 'Brij Bhasha', the language spoken around Delhi and Agra, mixed with the different Indian dialects such as Rajasthani, Punjabi, and even Persian. Although Kabir had a rich fund of intuitive wisdom and poetic talent, he was not a man of erudition. No wonder, his images and metaphors, like his diction, are derived from personal experience and observation of life.

It may also be remembered that apart from the influence of Vedantic thought, Kabir had also absorbed the influence of the Muslim sufi saints who are never tired of preaching the value of love, compassion and self-realisation. They had a firm faith in the oneness of God and the brotherhood of man. Kabir is, deservedly, counted among the saint-singers of India, and his "dohas," are a storehouse of wisdom and enlightenment. His dohas are available in: Kabir Granthavali, Sant Kabir, and Bijak.

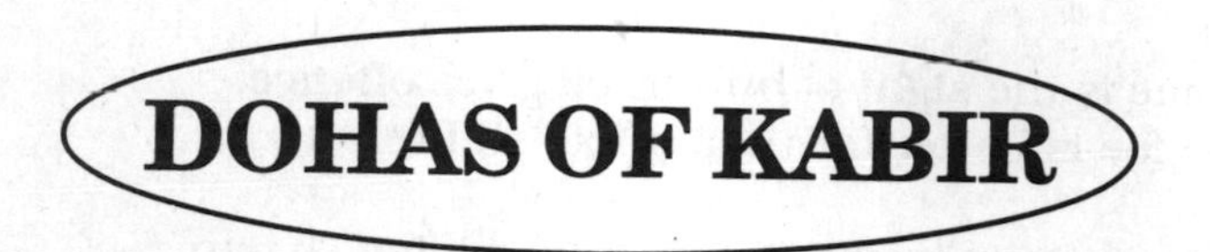

I have nothing to call my own, all is yours, O Lord,
If I return what you gave, I incur no loss.

Deep embedded is your grace in everything, O, Lord,
Like the henna's ruddy hue, ingrained in leaf and bark.

He who sought has found Thee, plumbing waters deep,
I, the stupid, sat on shore, afraid to wet my feet.

Everyone is eager to befriend the rich and great,
True friendship, says Kabir, is careless of rank or state.

With every breath you take, repeat His sacred name,
Who knows if the breath exhaled will ever come again.

Truth is the highest good, greed, the greatest crime,
Knowledge is the wealth unmatched, mind the sacred shrine.

Welcome is the sight of butter, oil gives offence,
A wise foe is better far than a foolish friend.

*Mera mujh mein kuchh nahin, jo kuchh hai so tera,*
*Tera tujhko saunpta, kya laage hai meral!*

*Sahiba teri sahibi sab ghat rahi samaey,*
*Jeon mehndi ke paat mein laali lakhi na jaaey.*

*Jin khoja tin paya gahre pani paith,*
*Main bauri khojan chali, gai kinare baith.*

*Gunwanta aur daraw se preet karen sab koey,*
*Kabira paret woh jaaneye jo in se nayaari hoey.*

*Sawaas sawaas pai naam le, baratha sawaas mat khoey,*
*Na jaane us sawaas ka aawan hoey na hoey.*

*Lobh saris awgun nahin, tap nahin satya samaan,*
*Tirath nahin man shudhi sam,vidya sam dhanwaan.*

*Ghee ke tau darshan bhale, khana bhala na tel*
*Dana tau dushman bhala, moorakh ka kya mel!*

मेरा मुझमें कुछ नहीं, जो कुछ है सो तेरा।
तेरा तुझको सोंपता, क्या लागे है मेरा।।

साहिब तेरी साहिबी, सब घट रही समाय।
ज्यों महंदी के पात में, लाली लखी ना जाय।।

जिन खोजा तिन पाइया, गहिरे पानी पैठ।
मैं बौरी खोजन चली, गई किनारे बैठ।।

गुणवन्ता और द्रव्य से, प्रीति करे सब कोय।
कबिरा प्रीति वो जानिये, जो इनसे न्यारी होय।।

श्वास श्वास पै नाम ले, वृथा श्वास मत खोय।
ना जाने उस श्वास का, आवन होय न होय।।

लोभ सरिस अवगुण नहीं, तप नहीं सत्य समान।
तीर्थ नहीं मन शुद्धि सम, विद्या सम धनवान।।

घी के तो दर्शन भले, खाना भला न तेल।
दाना तो दुश्मन भला, मूरख का क्या मेल।।

Kabira, be thou humble like the lowly grass,
Tall grass will wilt and wither, the dwarf grass will last.

If seven seas serve as ink, tree as pens, earth as page,
Even then I cannot His merits enumerate.

Man dies but the lure of life and his lusts stay,
Eternal are our hopes and dreams, Kabir humbly says.

Like a winnowing fan acts the holy saint,
He blows away the chaff, preserves the healthy grain.

The crow makes no demands, nor cuckoo gives us aught,
But cuckoo, being honey-tongued, conquers every heart.

As fragrance lives inside the rose, God lives inside our heart,
Like the maddened musk deer, seek Him not in leaf and grass.

Meditate on God, the gracious, keep your mouth closed,
Open thou the gates of heart, shut the outer doors.

*Kabira nanhe ho raho jaisi nanhi doob,*
*Sabhi ghaas jal jaaenge, doob khoob ki khoob.*

*Saat samd ki mas karoon, sab lekhni banraaey,*
*Kaagid sab dharti karoon, Hari gun likha na jaaey.*

*Maya mari na man mara mar mar gaye sharir,*
*Asha tarishna na mari kah gaye daas Kabir.*

*Sadhu aisa chaaheye jaisa soop sumaey,*
*Saar saar ko gahi rahe, thotha dey uraey.*

*Kaga kako dhan harey, koel kako det,*
*Meethe shabd sunaey ke, jag apna kar let.*

*Tera saaein tujhi mein pahupan mein baas,*
*Kastoori ka hiran jeon phirphir dhoondat ghaas.*

*Sumrat surat lagaey kar mukh se kuchh na bol,*
*Bahar ka pat dey kar ander ka pat khol.*

कबीरा नन्हे हो रहो, जैसी नन्ही दूब।
सभी घास जल जायेंगे, दूब खूब की खूब॥

सात समद की मसि करो, सब लेखनी बनराय।
कागद सब धरती करों, हरिगुन लिखा न जाय॥

माया मरी न मन मरा, मर मर गये शरीर।
आशा तृष्णा ना मरी, कह गये दास कबीर॥

साधू ऐसा चाहिए, जैसा सूप सुभाय।
सार सार को गहि रहै थोथा देय उड़ाय॥

कागा काको धन हरे, कोयल काको देत।
मीठे शब्द सुनाय के, जग अपना कर लेत॥

तेरा सांई तुझी मैं पहुपन में बास।
कस्तूरी का हिरण ज्यों, फिर फिर ढूंढत घास॥

सुमरत सुरत लगाय कर, मुख से कुछ ना बोल।
बाहर का पट देय कर, अन्दर का पट खोल॥

Love your God with all your heart, as a lover loves his mate,
Forget Him not for little while, hug Him tight in every state.

We pray to God when in trouble, but not in happier time,
Why should sorrows frighten us, if we pray when days are fine.

You may live on holy Ganges, drink its waters deep,
But till you link yourself with God, you cannot be at peace.

He for whom you search the world, resides within your heart,
The illusory veil warps your vision, so you miss the mark.

Ram devotees are engaged in contemplation deep,
But like the mirrorred beauty their goal escapes their reach.

Great is he who worships God, be he a slave or sire,
Greater still is he, O Kabir, who worships sans desire.

Repeated bathing cannot wash your lusts and greeds,
The fish stinks all the same, though submerged in seas.

*Sumrin se man laaeye jaise kaami kaam,*
*Ek palak bisre nahin nisdin aathon yaam.*

*Dukh mein sumrin sab kare, sukh mein kare na koey,*
*Jo sukh mein sumrin kare tau dukh kaahe ko hoey.*

*Ganga tir jo ghar kare, peewe nirmal neer,*
*Bin hari sumrin mukt na, kah gaye daas Kabir.*

*Ja kaaran jag dhoondia o tau hirday maahein,*
*Parda diya bharam ka tohe soojhe naahin.*

*Jo matwaare Ram ke lagan hue man maanh,*
*Jeon darpan ki sundari kinhoon pakra naanh.*

*Raja, Rani, Rank sab bara jo sumre naam,*
*Kah Kabir banda bara jo sumre nishkaam.*

*Nahaey dhoey kya hua jo man mein meil samaey,*
*Meen sada jal mein rahe dhoey baas na jaaey.*

सुमरन से मन लाइये, जैसे कामी काम।
एक पलक बिसरे नहीं, निसदिन आठों याम॥

दुख में सुमिरन सब करे, सुख में करे न कोय।
जो सुख में सुमिरन करे, तो दुख काहे को होय॥

गंगा तीर जो घर करै, पीवे निर्मल नीर।
बिन हरि सुमरिन मुक्ति ना, कह गये दास कबीर॥

जा कारण जग ढंढया, सो तो हृदय माहिं।
पर्दा दिया भरम का, तोहे सूझे नाहि॥

जो मतवारे राम के, लगन हुए मन मांह।
ज्यों दर्पण की सुन्दरी, किनहुं पकड़ा नांह॥

राजा, रानी, रंक सब, बड़ा जो सुमरे नाम।
कह कबीर बंदा बड़ा, जो सुमरे निष्काम॥

नहाये धोये क्या हुआ, जो मन में मैल समाय।
मीन सदा जल में रहै, धोये बास न जाय॥

Those who are honey-tongued but vicious at heart,
Are worse than stupid simpletons, uncouth, untaught.

Kabira wake up from your sleep, remember Krishan Murar,
The day will come when you'll sleep never to wake at all.

For long you have been telling beads, still your mind is evil-fraught,
Abandon ye the beads in hand, turn the beads in heart.

A droplet falling into the sea is seen by one and all,
That a drop conceals the sea, oft goes unmarked.

Wrapped in total ignorance, how can you find the path?
When a blind meets the blind, the result is chaos.

Despite making a million bows, despite visiting shrines,
You cannot make the spiritual leap unless by holy saints refined.

Priceless is the gift of speech, provided that you know the art,
Before you turn your thought to speech, weigh every word in your heart.

Ensure that your speech is free from hurtful pride and hate,
It should soothe the listener's heart with its gentle grace.

*Mukh ki meethi jo kahen hirday hai kumiti aan,*
*Kah Kabir tahi log se Ramu bara seaan.*

*Kabira sota kya hare jago japo muraar,*
*Ek din hai sovna laambe panw pisaar.*

*Mala pherat jag bhaya mita na man ka pher,*
*Karka manka chhor ke manka manka pher.*

*Boondpari samudr mein tahi jaane sab koey,*
*Samudr samaan boond mein birla boojhe koey.*

*Jana nahin boojha nahin, samajh gaya nahin gaun,*
*Andhe ko andha mila raah bataawe kaun!*

*Koti koti teerath kare, koti koti rahe dhaam,*
*Jab lag saadhan mein nahin tab lag kaacha kaam.*

*Boli tau anmol hai jo koi jaane bol,*
*Hirday taraazoo tol kar tab mukh baahir khol.*

*Aisi baani boleye man ka aapa khoey,*
*Auron ko sheetal kare, aapo sheetal hoey.*

मुख की मीठी जो कहें हृदय है कुर्मात आन।
कह कबीर तेहि लोग से रामू बड़ा सियान।।

कबीरा सोता क्या करे जागो जपो मुरार।
एक दिना है सोवना लांबे पांव पसार।।

माला फेरत जुग भया, मिटा न मन का फेर।
करका मनका छोड़ के मनका मनका फेर।।

बूंद पड़ी जो समुद्र में ताहि जाने सब कोय।
समुद्र समान बूंद में बिरला बूझे कोय।।

जाना नहीं बूझा नहीं समझ गया नहीं गौन।
अन्धे को अन्धा मिला राह बतावे कौन।।

कोटि कोटि तीर्थ करे कोटि कोटि रहे धाम।
जब लग साधन में नहीं तब लग काचा काम।।

बोली तो अनमोल है जो कोई जाने बोल।
हृदय तराजू तोल कर तब मुख बाहर खोल।।

ऐसी बानी बोलिए मन का आपा खोय।
औरों को शीतल करे आपौ शीतल होय।।

What use being big and tall like the palm tree,
No shade for the traveller, nor fruit within reach.

Mercy leads to godliness, greed taints the mind,
Anger has the seed of death, forgiveness is divine.

Human life is a gift of God, only once bestowed,
When a ripe fruit doth fall, it cannot be restored,

Our mind is like the juggler's ape, playing tricks galore,
It fascinates our senses, but strays us from the goal.

No use being a saint if your speech is uncontrolled,
If your words are bitter gall, and your tongue a sword.

If you get it in your head to slit someone's soul,
Remember he'll spare you not, beware his revengeful blow.

Wine robs us of our wits, 'tis a thing accursed,
Turns a man into an ass, drains away his purse.

*Bara hua tau kya hua jaise lamba khajoor,*
*Panchhi ko chhaya nahin phal laage ati door.*

*Jahan daya tahan dharm hai jahan lobh tahan paap,*
*Jahan karodh tahan kaal hai jahan shima tahan aap.*

*Maanush janam durlabh hai hue na dooji baar,*
*Pakka phal jo gir para lage na dooji baar.*

*Bazigar ka bandra aisa jeev man ke saath,*
*Nana nautch dikhaey kar raakhe apne haath.*

*Sadhu bhaey tau kya bhaey jo nahin bol vichar,*
*Hane parai atma jeev lieye talwar.*

*Kahta hoon kah jaat hoon kahe jo man hamaar,*
*Ja ko gala tum kaat ho, wah kaate tumhaar.*

*Awgun kahoon sharab ka aapa ahmaq hoey,*
*Maanush e pashua kare, daam gaanth se khoey.*

बड़ा हुआ तो क्या हुआ जैसे पेड़ खजूर।
पंछी को छाया नहीं फल लागे अति दूर।।

जहां दया तहां धर्म है जहां लोभ तहां पाप।
जहां क्रोध तहां काल है जहां छिपा तहां आप।।

मानुष जन्म दुर्लभ है हुए न दूजी बार।
पक्का फल जो गिर पड़ा लगे न दूजी बार।।

बाजीगर का बांदरा ऐसा जीव मन के साथ।
नाना नाच दिखाय कर राखे अपने हाथ।।

साधु भये तो क्या भये जो नहि बोल विचार।
हने पराई आत्मा जीभ लिये तलवार।।

कहता हूं कह जात हूं कहा जो मन हमार।
जाको गला तुम काट हो वह काटे तुम्हार।।

अवगुन कहूं शराब का आपा अहमक होय।
मानुष से पशुआ करें दाम गांठ से खोय।।

God and the guru, both are present, at whose feet to fall,
All praise to the guru, he made me see the Lord.

None is higher, O Kabir, than Guru, the great,
Nothing can you gain in life without the guru's grace.

Sour, sweet, and spicy, the greedy tongue craves,
When dog and thief conspire, who will guard the gate?

Rouse a saint from slumber sweet, so that he may pray,
But better let them lie asleep: the sinner, lion, or snake.

The brave do not flee the field in spite of heavy odds,
Unconcerned with life or death, they press on with their task.

Why complain about your hunger, why beseech and beg,
He who gave you mouth and belly, will also give you bread.

Doctor dies, patient dies, the whole world will pass,
He alone can conquer death who seeks refuge in God.

*Guru Govind dono khare kake laagon paaen,*
*Balihari guru apne Govind deo milaey.*

*Kabir teen lok navkhand mein guru te bara na koey,*
*Karta kar na kar sake, guru kare so hoey.*

*Khatta hatta chirchira jeebha sab ras lay,*
*Chor aur kutta mil gaya pehra kiska daey.*

*Sota sadhu jagaeye karen naam ka jaap,*
*Yeh teenon sote bhale: seekit, sinh aur saanp.*

*Khet na chhore shoorma, jhooje do dal maaheen,*
*Asha jeevan maran ki man mein rakhe naaheen.*

*Bhooka bhooka kya kare, kaha sunaaey log,*
*Bhanda gaad nij mukh diya soi pooran jog.*

*Vaid muva, rogi muva, muva sakal sansaar,*
*Ek Kabira na muva jehi ke Ram adhaar.*

गुरु गोबिन्द दोनों खड़े, काके लागौं पाँय।
बलिहारी गुरु आपने, गोविन्द दियो मिलाय।।

तीन लोक नव खंड में गुरु ते बड़ा न कोय।
करता कर न कर सके, गुरु करे सो होय।।

खट्टा हट्टा चिड़ चिड़ा जीभा सब रस लेय।
चोर और कुत्ता मिल गया पहरा किसका देय।।

सोता साधु जगाइए करें नाम का जाप।
यह तीनों सोते भले सीकित, सिंह और सांप।।

खेत न छोड़े शूरमा झुझें दो दल माहि।
आशा जीवन मरन की मन में रखे नाहिं।।

भूका भूका क्या करे कहां सुनाय लोग।
भांडा गाड़ निज मुख दिया सोई पूर्ण जोग।।

वैद्य मुवा रोगी मुवा मुवां सकल संसार।
एक कबीर ना मुवा जेहि के राम अधार।।

God can do whatever He wants, man is weak and vain,
God can change a mount to a hill, make it mount again.

Like a potter patting the pot, made of tender lay,
God loves us deep inside, slaps us on the face.

A loving heart is prized the most, whatever be your garb,
You may roam in distant wilds, or at home resort.

Everyone proclaims love, what is love? None knows,
True love is a ceaseless river that for ever flows.

The worldly riches are a cheat, which all the world defrauds,
He who robs this elfish temptress, deserves true applause.

As iris in the eye, God lives in the heart of man,
Due to sheer ignorance, we cannot understand.

Never should you beg or cringe, begging brings disgrace,
Prefer death to begging, thus opine the sage.

*Saaein se sab hot hai, bande se kuchh naaen,*
*Rye se parbat kare, parbat rye naaen.*

*Kaache bhande se rahe jeon kumhaar ka neh,*
*Bheetar se raksha kare, baahir choten del.*

*Prem bhav ik chaaheye bhes anek banaey,*
*Chaahe ghar mein vaas kare, chaahe ban kojaaey.*

*Prem prem sab koi kahe, preet na jaane koey,*
*Aath pahar bahta rahe prem kahawe soey.*

*Maya tau thagni bani, thagat phire sab desh,*
*Ja thag ne thagni thagi, tau thag ko aadesh.*

*Jeon nainon mein putli teon malik ghat maanh,*
*Moorakh log na jaaneye baahir dhoondan jaaey.*

*Maangan maran samaan hai mat koi maango bheekh,*
*Maangan se marna bhala yeh sadguru ki seekh.*

सांई से सब होत है बंदे से कुछ नांय।
राई से पर्वत करे पर्वत राई नांह।।

काचे भाँडे से रहे ज्यों कुम्हार का नेह।
भीतर से रक्षा करे, बाहिर चोटें देय।।

प्रेम भाव इक चाहिए भेष अनेक बनाय।
चाहे घर में वास करे चाहे बन को जाय।।

प्रेम प्रेम सब कोई कहे प्रीत न जाने कोय।
आठ पहर बहता रहे प्रेम कहावे सोय।।

माया तो ठगनी बनी ठगत फिरे सब देश।
जा ठग ने ठगनी ठगी तो ठग को आदेश।।

ज्यों नैनों में पुतली त्यों मालिक घर मांह।
मूर्ख लोग न जानिए बाहिर ढ़ंढन जांय।।

मांगन मरन समान है मत कोई मांगो भीख।
मांगन से मरना भला यह सद्गुरु की सीख।।

Questing Ram in the wilds without a proper spiritual guide,
Is to make a wild goose chase, bound to prove futile.

Ugly, dark, dun or shabby, a faithful wife is better far,
Than a paragon of beauty, faithless to her wedded lord.

Your hand may tell the beads, your tongue His name repeat,
If your mind wanders still, you'll miss the spiritual meed.

A saint, a tree, a water tank, and a shower of rain,
All the four are born to serve without an eye on gain.

Harping on "you" and "me" has torn the world to bits,
But those firmly entrenched in faith, no such rift admit.

Among the gifts food is best, among the names, the best is God's,
Humility is the best of virtue, pride, the greatest fault.

He who treats sleep as smoke,ignores abuse, conquers rage,
Such a man, says Kabir, is the real sage.

*Ram rahe ban bheetare, guru ki na pooji aas,*
*Kahe Kabir, paakhand sab, jhoote sada niraas*

*Pativrata maili bhali, kali, kuchal, karoop,*
*Pativrata ke roop par waaroon kot saroop.*

*Mala kar mein phire, jeebh phire mukh maanh,*
*Manua tau dash dishe phire, yeh tau sumrin naanh.*

*Taruwar, sarwar, sant jan, chauthe barse meinh,*
*Parmarath ke kaarne chaaron dhaaren deh.*

*Mor tor ki jeevari bant baandha sansaar,*
*Kabira kyon daas bandhe jake naam aadhaar!*

*Lene ko sat naam hai, dene ko ann daan,*
*Tirne ko hai deenata, dooban ko abhimaan.*

*Gaar agaar karodh jal, nindia dhuaan hoey,*
*In teenon ko parhare saadh kahawe soey.*

राम रहे बन भीतरे गुरु की न पूजी आस।
कहे कबीर पाखंड सब, झूठे सदा निरास॥

पतिवरता मैली भली काली कुचल कुरूप।
पतिवरता के रूप पर बारूं कोट सरूप॥

माला कर मैं फिरे जीभ फिरे मुख मांह।
मनुआं तो दश दिशे फिरे यह तो सुमरण नांह॥

तरूवर सरवर संत जन चौथे बरसे मेह।
परमारथ के कारणे चारों धारें देह॥

मोर तोर की जीवरी बंट बांधा संसार।
कबीरा क्यों दास बंधे जाके नाम आधार॥

लेने को सत नाम है देने को अन्न दान।
तिरने को है दीनता डूबन को अभिमान॥

गार अगार क्रोध जल, निंदिया धूआं होय।
इन तीनों को परहरे साध कहावे सोय॥

Man's life is a water-bubble, it will soon dissolve,
It will vanish unperceived, like the morning star.

A single abuse, if returned, gets multiplied,
But it remains fixed as one, if not replied.

Sleep is better than wakefulness, only if you know the art,
Seal yourself from the world around, meditate on God.

Enlightenment is what you need, all the world is dust,
Kabira came, surveyed the scene, departed in disgust.

He whose heart is averse to truth, tongue is uncontrolled,
Such a man's company brings regrets untold.

Our body is the venomous vine, guru the nectar's mine,
No price is too great to win his grace benign.

If you stand estranged from God, beseech the guru's aid,
But God will reject you if guru you alienate.

*Pani ka hai bulbula is maanas ki jaat,*
*Dekhat hi chhip jaaenge jeon tara parbhat.*

*Aawat gaali ek hai, ulte hot anek,*
*Kahen Kabir nahin ultieye, wahi ek ki ek.*

*Jaagan se sovan bhala, jo koi jaane soey*
*Ander lau laagi rahe, sahjan samran hoey.*

*Gian ratan ka jatan karo, maati ka sansaar,*
*Aya Kabira, phir gaya, pheeka hai sansaar.*

*Jake jeebia bandhan nahin, hirday nahin saanch,*
*Bake sang na laageye, khale batia kaanch.*

*Yeh tan vish ki belri, guru amrit ki khaan,*
*Sis dieyejo guru mile, tau bhi sasta jaan.*

*Kabira Hari ke roothte, guru ke sarne jaaey,*
*Kah Kabir guru roothte, Hari nahin hot sahaey.*

पानी का है बुलबुला इस मानस की जात।
देखत ही छुप जायेंगे ज्यों तारा प्रभात।।

आवत गाली एक है उलटे होत अनेक।
कहे कबीर नहीं उलटिये वही एक ही एक।।

जागन से सोवन भला जो कोई जाने सोय।
अन्दर लौ लागी रहे सहजन स्मरण होय।।

ज्ञान रतन का जतन करो माटी का संसार।
आया कबीरा फिर गया फीका है संसार।।

जाके जिभ्या बंधन नहीं हृदय नाही सांच।
वाके संग न लागिए खाले बटिया कांच।।

यह तन विष की बेलरी, गुरु अमृत की खान।
सीस दिए जो गुरु मिलें, तो भी सस्ता जान।।

कबीरा हरि के रूठते, गुरु के सरने जाय।
कह कबीर गुरु रूठते, हरि नहीं होत सहाय।।

Swans do not strut in flocks, nor lions move in droves,
Rubies aren't stacked in sacks, saints do not rove in rows.

A saint carries no packs beyond what he eats,
God is there to help him and supply his needs.

You spend your day in eating, in slumber goes your night,
You cast away for nothing the precious gem of life.

Judge not a saint by his class, but by his spiritual lore,
Forget about the scabbard, settle for the sword.

You, O Lord, are my prop, you are my anchor-sheet,
Like a crow around the mast, I circle round your feet.

Many an evil deed I did, undeterred by aught,
You may kill me if you like, or my sins absolve.

Seek the company of the saints, do not vacillate, .
It will help dispel your vice, virtue stimulate.

*Sehon ke lenhre nahin, hanson ki nahin paant,*
*Lalon ki nahin boriaan, saadh na chalejamaat.*

*Sadhu gaanthi na baandhai, udar samata lay,*
*Aage peechhe Hari khare, Jab maange tab day.*

*Raat ganwaai soe kaar, divas ganwaya khaey,*
*Hira janam anmol tha, kauri badle jaaey.*

*Jaati na poochho saadh ki, poochh lijeye gian,*
*Mol karo talwaar ka, para rahn do mayaan.*

*Sahib tumhin dayal ho turn lag meri daur,*
*Jaise kaagjahaaz ko, mujhe aur na thor.*

*Avgun kieye tau bahu kieye, kart na maani haar,*
*Bhanven banda baksieye, bhanven gardan maar.*

*Kabira sangat saadh ki, begi karjejaai Jaaey,*
*Durmati door ganwaisi, desi sumiti hataaey.*

सिहों के लेंहडे नहीं, हंसों की नहि पाँत।
लालों की नहिं बोरियां, साध न चलें जमात।।

साधू गाँठि न बाँधई, उदर समाता लेय।
आगे पीछे हरि खड़े, जब माँगे तब देय।।

रात गँवाई सोय कर, दिवस गँवाया खाय।
हीरा जन्म अमोल था, कौड़ी बदले जाय।।

जाति न पूछो साध की, पूछ लीजिए ज्ञान।
मोल करौ तलवार का, पड़ा रहन दो म्यान।।

साहब तुमहि दयाल हौ, तुम लागे मेरी दौर।
जैसे काग जहाज को, सूझै और न ठौर।।

औगुन किए तो बहु किए, करत न मानी हार।
भावै बंदा बकसिए, भावै गरदन मार।।

कबिरा संगत साध की, बेगि करीजै जांइ।
दुरमति दूरि गँवाइसी, देसी सुमति बताइ।।

Do not spurn even a straw lying beneath your feet,
It may blow into your eye, causing agony deep.

Do not get drunk with pride, death awaits us all,
Who knows when and where the fatal blow may fall.

We take delight in mundane things, take false for true,
We all serve as food for death, some he spares, some he chews.

As you sow you must inevitably reap,
Those who plant brambles, mangoes cannot eat.

The disciple should offer all he has at the guru's feet,
The guru should give his grace gratis without charging fees.

Even if, like the fish, you hide yourself beneath the sea,
The death with its dragnet wide will trap and devour thee.

A tug-of-war is going on betwist mind and soul,
In this dilly-dallying, we miss the cherished goal.

*Tinka kabhoon na nindeye, jo paayan tar hoey,*
*Kabhunke uri aankhan pare, pir ghaneri hoey.*

*Kabira garbh na kijeye kaal gahe kar kes,*
*Na jaano kit maarihai, kya ghar kya pardes.*

*Jhute sukh ko sukh kahen maanat hai man modh,*
*Jagat chabena kaal ka, kuchh mukh mein, kuchh godh.*

*Karta tha so kyon kiya, ab kar kyon pachhtaey,*
*Boya per babool ka aam kahan se khaey!*

*Sikh ko aisa chaaheye guru ko sar bas de,*
*Guru ko aisa chaaheye sikh ka kuchh na le.*

*Machh bhaye na baanchi, ho dhimar tera kaal,*
*Jaihi -jaihi davar tu phire, tahan tahan milejaal.*

*Man tau kahe kahan jaaeye, chit kahe kahan jaoon,*
*Chhe maas ke hatyat adha kos base gaon.*

तिनका कबहुँ न निन्दिए, जो पायन तर होय।
कबहुँक उड़ि आँखन परै, पीर धनेरी होय।।

कबिरा गर्व न कीजिए, काल गहे कर केस।
न जानौं कित मारिहै, क्या घर क्या परदेस।।

झूठे सुख को सुख कहें, मानत है मन मोद।
जगत चबेना काल का, कुछ मुख में कुछ गोद।।

करता था सो क्यों किया, अब कर क्यों पछताय।
बोया पेड़ बबूल का, आम कहां से खाय।।

सिख को ऐसा चाहिये गुरु को सरबस दे।
गुरु को ऐसा चाहिये सिख का कुछ ना ले।।

मच्छ भये न बांची हो धीमर तेरा काल।
जेहि-जेहि डावर तू फिरे तहाँ तहाँ मिले जाल।।

मन तो कहैं कहां जाइए चित कहें कहां जाऊँ।
छैः मास के हटयत अधा कोस बसे गांव।।

Water doesn't upward climb, but down the slope flows,
The haughty heads go athirst, he only drinks who bows.

Take a bucketful from the river, the river flows brimful still,
Wealth doesn't deplete at all, give in charity as you will.

They who drink the wine of love, are not afraid to die,
The bliss of love is not for them who shrink from sacrifice.

Burn away your hopes, eschew all desire,
If you want to kindle the true celestial fire.

As oil in the linseed, fire in the stone,
So is God within us, let this truth be known.

Body is a boat, mind a crow, given to sudden flights,
Now sinking in the sea of doubt, now soaring in the sky.

Ten-gated is the prison where breath lies encaged,
Wonder why it lies confined, no wonder it escapes.

*Oonche paani ka tike, neeche di thahraey,*
*Neecha ho so bhare paey, ooncha pyasa jaaey.*

*Daan diey dhan na ghate, nadi na ghaate neer,*
*Apni aankho dekh lo, yon kahen das Kabir.*

*Prem payala jo pieye, sees dakshina dey,*
*Lobhi sheesh na de sake, naam prem ka ley.*

*Asha ka eendhan karo, mansa karo babhoot,*
*Jogi pheri yon karo tab ban aawe soot.*

*Jeon til maahein tel hai, jeon chakmak mein aag,*
*Tera maalik tujhi mein jaag sake tau jaag.*

*Tan bohat man kaag hai,laksh yojan ur jaaey,*
*Kabhun bharm nahin, kabhun na gagan samaaey.*

*Das dwaar ka pinjara ta mein panchhi paun,*
*Rahe ko acharaj hot hai, gaye achamba kaun.*

ऊंचे पानी का टिके नीचे दी ठहराय।
नीचा हो सो भरे पये ऊंचा प्यासा जाय।।

दान दिये धन ना घटे नदी न घाटे नीर।
अपनी आंखों देख लो यों कहें दास कबीर।।

प्रेम प्याला जो पिये सीस दक्षिणा देय।
लोभी शीश न दे सके नाम प्रेम का लेय।।

आशा का ईंधन करो मनसा करो बभूत।
जोगी फेरी यों करो तब बन आवे सूत।।

ज्यों तिल मांहि तेल है ज्यों चकमक में आग।
तेरा मालिक तुझी में जाग सके तो जाग।।

तन बोहत मन काग है लक्ष योजन उड़ जाय।
कबहूँ भर्म अगम नहीं कबहूँ न गगन समाय।।

दस द्वारे का पींजरा ता मैं पंछी पौन।
रहे को अचरज होत है गये अचंभा कौन।।

Gold, saint, and a noble mind, break and join again,
Petty minds, like the potter's pot, once cracked, cracked remain.

Absorb yourself in God like the fish submerged in sea,
Sunder it from water, lo, it cannot breathe.

We can judge a saint or sinner from the way he speaks,
A sure index of the mind is our mode of speech.

High birth, unmatched with deeds, loses native shine,
Gold goblet begins to stink if filled with wine.

We have said everything, nothing more to say,
The One remains, the many die, swept under the wave.

Much of our time goes in business, the rest in slumber deep,
We cannot spare a minute for prayer, how can we garner peace?

Minute by minute your body dies, do something apace,
Serve thou the holy saints, learn to meditate.

*Sona, sajjan, saadh jan, toot jure sau baar,*
*Durjan, kumbh, kumhar ka eke dhakka daraar.*

*Sumran se man laaeye jaise paani meen,*
*Pran taje chhin bichhre, sant Kabir kah deen.*

*Bani se pahchaaneye sahu chor ki jaat,*
*Ander ki karni sabe nikle munh ki baat.*

*Oonche kul mein janmia karni oonch na hoey,*
*Sauran kalash sura bhari sadhu ninda hoey.*

*Kahna tha so kah chale ab kuchh kaha najaaey,*
*Ek raha dooja gaya, darya lahr samaey.*

*Paanch pahar dhande gaya, teen pahr gaya soey,*
*Ekpahr Hari naam bin, mukti kaise hoey?*

*Kya bharosa deh ka, bins jaat chhin maanh,*
*Saans saans sumran karo, aur yatan kuchh naanh.*

सोना, सज्जन, साध जन, टूट जुड़े सौ बार।
दुर्जन कुम्भ कुम्हार का एके धक्का दरार॥

सुमरण से मन लाइये जैसे पानी मीन।
प्राण तजे छिन बिछड़े, संत कबीर कह दीन॥

बानी से पहचानिये साहू चोर की जात।
अन्दर की करनी सबै निकले मुँह की बात॥

ऊंचे कुल में जन्म्या करनी ऊंच न होय।
सौरन कलश सुरा भरी साधू निन्दा होय॥

कहना था सो कह चले अब कुछ कहा न जाय।
एक रहा दूजा गया दरिया लहर समाय॥

पांच पहर धन्धे गया तीन पहर गया सोय।
एक पहर हरि नाम बिन मुक्ति कैसे होय॥

क्या भरोसा देह का बिनस जात छिन मांह।
सांस-सांस सुमरण करों और यतन कुछ नांह॥

Beware the sudden swoop of death, do no evil deeds,
You cannot reap the harvest, unless you sow the seed.

Revere thy guru day and night, he is your guide to God,
Without his grace the house of heart remains plunged in dark.

Oblivious of the goal of life you are slumbering deep,
Realize youself, O sluggard, wake up from your sleep.

Ego breeds agony, doubt begets disease,
How to overcome these ills, baffles Bhagat Kabir

Illusory is the glittering wealth, but few realize this truth,
It follows them who spurn it, shuns them who pursue.

Deadly is the poor man's curse, fatal to your weal,
Like the bellow's silent breath, which can melt the steel.

Eat, drink, and spend your riches, enjoy every bit,
Nothing will you carry along when this world you quit.

*Kaal kaal tatkaal hai bura na kareye koe,*
*An bowe lunta nahin, bowe lunta hoe.*

*So guru nisdin bandiey jaason paya Ram,*
*Naam bina ghat andh hai jeon deepak bin dhaam.*

*Aya tha kis kaam ko tu soya chadar taan,*
*Surat sambhal, ai ghafil, apna aap pahchaan.*

*Jahan aapa tahan aapda,jahan sanshay tahan rog,*
*Kah Kabir yeh kyon miten, chaaron niradh rog.*

*Maya chhaya eksi birla jaane koe,*
*Bhagtaan ke paachhe lage, sanmukh bhage soe.*

*Durbal ko na sataeye, jaki moti haae,*
*Bina jeev ki saans se loha bhasm ho jaaey.*

*Khaaey pakaey lutaae ke, kar le apna kaam,*
*Chalti biriya re nar sang na chale chhadaam.*

काल काल तत्काल है, बुरा न करिये कोय।
अन बोवे लुनता नहीं, बोवे लुनता होय।।

सो गुरु निस दिन बंदिये जासों पाया राम।
नाम बिना घट अंध है ज्यों दीपक बिना धाम।।

आया था किस काम को तू सोया चादर तान।
सूरत संभाल ऐ गाफिल अपना आप पहचान।।

जहां आपा तहां आपदा जहां संशय तहां रोग।
कह कबीर यह क्यों मिटे चारों नीरध रोग।।

माया छाया एक सी बिरला जाने काये।
भगतां के पाछे लगे सन्मुख्र भागे सोय।।

दुर्बल को न सताइये, जाकी मोटी हाय।
बिना जीव की सांस से, लोह भस्म हो जाय।।

खाय पकाय लुटाय के, करले अपना काम।
चलती बिरिया रे नर संग न चले छदाम।।

If someone pricks you with a thorn, pat him with a rose,
Good is its own reward, evil stings the soul.

Kashi, Kaaba , Ram, Rahim, are in fact the same,
The same dough produces sweets of different names.

The steel assumes different shapes put in different moulds,
Now it is the shield that guards, now the mortal sword.

Ride the elephant of knowledge, with patience overlaid,
The world is but a barking dog, let it bark and bay.

The buds raise a plaintive cry, seeing the flower-plucker approach,
To-morrow will he turn to us, to day he picks the blossoming rose.

The world is a lamp, man the moth, wheeling ill-content,
Blessed by the guru's grace, he can his fate transcend.

If getting our heads shaved could bring us nearer God,
The sheep shorn repeatedly would sure in heaven lodge.

*Jo toke kaanta bowe, tahi bowe tu phool,*
*Tahi phool ke phool hain, baaqi hain tirshul.*

*Kashi Kaaba ek hai, eke Ram, Rahim,*
*Maida ek pakwan bahu, baith Kabirajeem.*

*Kabira loha ek hai, gharne mein hai pher,*
*Taahin ka bakhtar bana, tahhin ki shamsher.*

*Hasti charheye gian ka sahj ghalicha daar,*
*Shwaan roop sansaar hai, bhaukan de jhakmaar.*

*Mali aawat dekh ke kalian kari pukar,*
*Phooli phooli chun liey kal hamari baar.*

*Maya deepak, narpatang, bharami bharami evai parant,*
*Kahai Kabir guru gian se ek aap ubrant.*

*Mood mudaey Hari mile sab koi lai mudaey,*
*Bar bar ke mood se bher na baikunth jaaey.*

जो तोको कांटा बोवे, ताहि बोव तू फूल।
तोहि फूल के फूल हैं, वाको हैं तिरसूल।।

काशी काबा एक है, एकै राम रहीम।
मैदा एक पकवान बहु, बैठ कबीरा जीम।।

कबीर लोहा एक है, घड़ने में है फेर।
ताही का बख्तर बना, ताही की समसेर।।

हस्ती चढ़िए ज्ञान का सहज गलीचा डार।
श्वान रूप संसार है भौंकन दे झक मार।।

माली आवत देख के कलियन करी पुकार।
फूली-फूली चुन लिए कल हमारी बार।।

माया, दीपक, नर, पतंग भ्रमि-भ्रमि इवै पड़न्त।
कहै कबीर गुरु ज्ञान से एक आप उबरन्त।।

मूड़ मुड़ाए हरि मिलें, सब कोई लेइ मुड़ाय।
बार-बार के मूड़ ते, भेड़ न बैकुंण्ठ जाय।।

Befuddled is the world's vision, it can't tell a saint from thief,
He who has a score of followers is crowned the head priest.

He who feels the others' pain is the holy priest,
Infidel is he who's blind to the other's grief.

Kabir couldn't contain his tears seeing the grinding mill rotate,
Caught betwist the twin stones, none can come out safe.

Despite wearing spotless clothes, and chewing betel leaf,
Without devotion to the Lord, you can't escape inferno's heat.

If the waters flood your boat, excess wealth your home invades,
Bale them out with both your hands, this is how you can be saved.

All are the forms of God, the myriad shapes on earth,
God and being, like word and thought, lie closely merged.

No God where lust resides, lust the sight of God flies,
Never can they co-exist, shining sun and sable night.

*Phooti aankh bibek ki, lakhe na sant, asant,*
*Jake sang dass bees hain, ta ko naam mahant.*

*Kabira soi pir hai jo jaanepar pir,*
*Jo par pir na janeye so kafir be pir.*

*Chalti chakki dekh ke diya Kabira roey,*
*Dooi pat bheetar aai ke sabit gaya na koey.*

*Ujjval pahre kapra, paan supari khaaey,*
*Ek Hari ke naam bin, baandha yampur jaaey.*

*Jo jal baarhe naav mein, ghar mein baarhe daam,*
*Dou haath ulecheye, yeh sajjan ko kaam.*

*Hari ka bana saroop sab, jeta yeh aakaar,*
*Akshar arth yon bhakheye, kahe Kabir vichar.*

*Jahan kaam tahan naam nahin,jahan naam kahan kaam,*
*Donon kabhun nahin mile, ravi rajni ek tham.*

फूटी आंख्र बिवेक की लख्रे न सन्त असन्त।
जाके संग दस बीस हैं ताको नाम महन्त।।

कबिरा सोई पीर है, जो जाने पर पीर।
जो पर पीर न जानई, सो काफिर बेपीर।।

चलती चक्की देखि के, दिया कबीरा रोय।
दुई पट भीतर आइ के साबित गया न कोय।।

उज्जवल पहरे कपड़ा, पान सुपारी ख्राय।
एक हरि के नाम बिन, बाँधा यमपुर जाय।।

जो जल बाढ़ें नाव में, घर में बाढ़ै दाम।
दोऊ हाथ उलीचिए, यह सज्जन को काम।।

हरि का बना सरूप सब, जेता यह आकार।
अच्छर अर्थ यों भाख्रिये, कहे कबीर विचार।।

जहां काम तहां नाम नहीं जहां नाम कहां काम।
दोनों कबहू नहीं मिले रवि रजनी एक ठाम।।

My Lord beloved met me in dream, woke me from my sleep,
I fear to open my eyes, lest I lose my darling sweet.

My Master has many virtues, all are on my heart engraved,
I fear to drink a glass of water, lest these virtues are effaced.

Come into my eyes, Lord, I'll close my eyelids tight,
Never will I lose your sight, nor let you see outside.

I have prepared this composition pilfering others' words and thoughts,
But how long can we live Kabir, on borrowed bread and stolen orts?

The clay tells the potter: why dost thou knead me so,
The day will come when I will knead you like the dough.

No foe can trouble a man whose heart is pure and kind,
Surrender but your ego, and the world will turn benign.

God grant me sufficient means to satisfy my family needs,
To appease my bodily hunger, the roving saints to feed.

*Supne mein saaein mile, sovat liya jagaey,*
*Aankh na kholoon darpata mat sapna hai jaaey.*

*Saaein mere bahut gun likhejo hirday maanheen,*
*Pind na paani darpata mat weh dhoey jaaen.*

*Nainon ander aaw tu, nain jhaanpe tohi leoon,*
*Na main dekhoon aur ko, na tohe dekhan deoon.*

*Laya saakhi kaat kar, it ut akshar kaat,*
*Kahe Kabir kab lag jieye, joothi pattal chaat!*

*Maati kahe kumhar se, tu kyon raundey moey,*
*Ik din aisa aaega, main raundoongi toey.*

*Jag mein beri koi nahin, jo man sheetal hoey,*
*Yeh aapa tau daal de, daya kare sab koey.*

*Saaein itana dijieye, jamein kutum samaey,*
*Main bhi bhooka na rahoon, saadhu na bhooka jaaey.*

सुपने में सांई मिले सोवत लिया जगाय।
आंख न खोलूं डरपता मत सपना है जाय॥

सांईं मेरे बहुत गुन लिखे जु हिरदे मांहि।
पिंड न पानी डरपता मत वे धोए जाहिं॥

नैनों अन्दर आव तू नैन झांपि तोहि लेऊं।
ना मैं देखूं और को न तेहि देखन देऊं॥

लाया साखी काट कर, इत उत अक्षर काट।
कहे कबीर कब लग जिए, जूठी पत्तल चाट॥

माटी कहे कुम्हार से, तू क्यों रौंदे मोय।
इक दिन ऐसा आएगा, मैं रौंदूगी तोय॥

जग मे बैरी कोई नहीं, जो मन शीतल होय।
यह आपा तो डाल दे, दया करे सब कोय॥

सांईं इतना दीजिए, जामें कुटुम समाय।
मैं भी भूखा न रहूँ, साधु न भूखा जाय॥

Even a dunce becomes clever with practice long and hard,
A rope running across the stone, cuts a groove at last.

The leaf fell from the tree, the wind blew it far,
Will it meet its parted mates, no one knows at all.

Kabir, your hamlet is located beside the hangmen's huts,
Those who slay will kiss the rod, why do you feel upset?

It's not a thing from books derived, but something actually seen with eyes,
The wedding party sheds its lustre, when the groom meets the bride.

When you chased your worldly goal, single-minded was your drive,
Break your bonds with the world, to become an acolyte.

Why do you turn us back and forth, say the wooden beads,
Turn, instead the beads of heart, if God you want to see.

I do not have the cheek, O Lord, to put my prayer across,
You can see my sinful deeds, you may cut me short.

*Karat karart abhyaas ke jarmati hot sujaan,*
*Rasri aawat jaat te, shil par hot nishaan.*

*Patta toota daal se, le gai pawan uraaey,*
*Ab ke bichhre kab milen, doori parenge jaaey.*

*Kabira teri jhaunpari gal-kattian ke paas,*
*Karan ge so bharan ge, tu kyon bhayo udaas?*

*Likha likhi ki hai nahin, dekha dekhi baat,*
*Dulha dulhan mil gaey, pheeki pari baraat.*

*Jab lagna tha jagat ka, tab lagbhag te na hoey,*
*Naata tore Hari bhaje, bhagat kahaawe soey.*

*Mala kahe hai kaath ki tu kyon phere moye,*
*Manka manka pher de, so turant mila doon toye.*

*Kya mukh hai binti karoon, laaj aawat hai moye.*
*Tum dekhat augun karun, kaise bhaun toye?*

करत करत अभ्यास के जड़मति होत सुजान।
रसरी आवत जावत ते सिल पर होत निसान।।

पत्ता टूटा डाल से ले गई पवन उड़ाय।
अब के बिछुरे न मिलें दूरि परेंगे जाय।।

कबीरा तेरी झोंपड़ी गल कटयन के पास।
करन गे सो भरण गे तू क्यों भयो उदास।।

लिखा लिखी की है नहीं देखा देखी बात।
दूल्हा दुलहन मिल गए फीकी पड़ी बरात।।

जब लगना था जगत का तब लगभग तेन होय।
नाता तोड़े हरि भजे भक्त कहावे सोय।।

माला कहै है काठ की तू क्यों फेरे मोय।
मन का मनका फेर दे सो तुरत मिला दूँ तोय।।

क्या मुख है बिनती करूँ लाज आवत है मोय।
तुम देखत औगुन करूँ कैसे भाऊँ तोय।।

For ever do they talk of "words", which nor have hands nor feet,
Yet one word could heal the wound, the other make us bleed.

Your hands tell the sacred beads, the tongue wags inside,
But the mind wanders everywhere, such worship cuts no ice.

In the wind of love that rose, skyward flew the straw,
It joined the other floating mates, reached its source at last.

In the room of my eye, with its pupil as the bed,
Eye-lids serving as a coverlet, with a loving gaze my Lord I fed.

Death which frightens one and all, fills me with delight,
When will it come and join me with the blissful font of light!

Happy is the world at large, it eats, sleeps, and snores,
Poor Kabir, who keeps awake, sighs and weeps full sore.

In vain I looked for someone bad in the world outside,
But when I looked within, I found none as bad as I.

*Sabad sabad sab koi kahe, sabad ke haath na paanv,*
*Ek sabad aushudh kare, ek sabad kari ghaav.*

*Mala tau kar mein phire, jeebh phire mukh maanhin,*
*Manav tau chahun dis phire, yeh tau sumran naahin.*

*Utha bagola prem ka tinka ura akash,*
*Tinka tinka se mila, tinka tin ke paas.*

*Nainan ki kar kothri, putri palang bichhaey,*
*Palkon ki chit dari ke, pi ko liya rijhae.*

*Ja marne se jag dare, mere man anand,*
*Kab marun, kab paaun, puran parmanand.*

*Sukhia sab sansaar hai, khaaey aur soey,*
*Dukhiya das Kabir hai, jaage aur roey.*

*Bura jo dekhan main chala, bura na milia koey,*
*Jo dil khoja aapna, tau mujh se bura na koey.*

सबद सबद सब कोई कहे, सबद के हाथ न पांव।
इक सबद अशुद्ध करे इक सबद करि घाव।।

माला तो कर में फिरे जीभ फिरे मुख्र मांहि।
मानव तो चहूँ दिस फिरे, ये तो सुमरण नाहिं।।

उठा बगोला प्रेम का तिनका उड़ा अकास।
तिनका तिनका से मिला, तिनका तिनके पास।।

नैनन की कर कोठरी पुतरी पलंग बिछाय।
पलकों की चित दरी के पी को लिया रिझाय।।

जा मरने से जग डरे मेरे मन आनन्द।
कब मरूँ कब पाऊँ पूरण परमानन्द।।

सुखिया सब संसार है खाये और सोय।
दुखिया दास कबीर है जागे और रोय।।

बुरा जो देखन मैं चला, बुरा न मिलिया कोय।
जो दिल खोजा आपना तो मुझसे बुरा न कोय।।

I adore one only God, of Him I think and dream,
If I think of another lord, it annoys the Lord supreme.

It is good my pot is broken, how relieved I feel!
No need to visit the well for water, to ply the rope and wheel.

It is the stern abode of love, and not your aunt's place
Get ready to stake your head, if here you would stay.

It is the redness of my Rose that fills the earth and sky,
I too went to see the show, and came back ruddy-dyed.

Kabira called the physician, and he felt my pulse,
But he couldn't detect the pain, for in the heart it lurked.

My Lord gave a loving call, but I couldn't oblige,
How could a bride, dirt-stained, meet her lover, spotless white!

He who calls you out of love, meet him without delay,
But better shrug off the man whose love is sham and fake.

*Sahib mera ek hai duja kaha na jaaey,*
*Duja sahib jo kahun, sahib khara ra saaey.*

*Bhala hua meri matki phooti re,*
*Main tau pania bharan se chhooti re.*

*Yeh tau ghar hai prem ka, khaala ka ghar naahin,*
*See utare bhuyen dhare tab baithe ghar maahin.*

*Lali mere lal ki, jit dekhun tit lal,*
*Lali dekhan main gai, main bhi ho gai lal.*

*Kabira baid bulaya pakad ke dekhi baanh,*
*Baid na vedan jaani karak kaleje maahin.*

*Yaar bulawe bhav sun, mope gaya na jaaey,*
*Dulhan maili piyu ujla, laag sakun na paae.*

*Het prem sau jo mile, ta ko milieye dhaaey,*
*Antar raakhe jo mile, taase mile balaaey.*

साहब मेरा एक है दूजा कहा न जाय।
दूजा साहब जो कहूँ साहब खड़ा रिसाय।।

भला हुआ मेरी मटकी फूटी रे।
मैं तो पनिया भरन से छूटी रे।।

यह तो घर है प्रेम का खाला का घर नाहिं।
सीस उतारें भुंये धरे तब बैठ घर माहिं।।

लाली मेरे लाल की जित देखूं तित लाल।
लाली देखन मैं गई मैं भी हो गई लाल।।

कबीरा बैद्य बुलाया पकड़ के देखी बांह।
बैद्य न बेदन जानि कड़क कलेजे मांहि।।

यार बुलावे भाव सों मोपे गया न जाये।
दुलहन मैली पियु उज्जला लागे सकों न पायें।।

हेत प्रेम सों जो मिले, ताको मिलिए धाय।
अन्तर राखे जो मिले तासे मिले बलाय।।

A saint seeks regard and reverence, not material wealth,
If he hungers after wealth, his saintly pose is a sheer pretext.

I am bonded with the One who lives in one and all,
All are mine, I am theirs, the otherness stands dissolved.

For long we sat Kabira, at the wine-distiller's shop,
Those who offered their head, alone could drink the draught.

Where to put the collyrium streak, whcre the vermilion mark,
With the Lord's image topped, where is the room for extras?

*Saadhu bhooka, bhaav ka, dhan ka bhooka naahin,*
*Dhan ka bhooka jo phire, so tau saadhu naahin.*

*Main laga uss ek se, ek bhaya sab maahin,*
*Sab mera main saban ka, tihan doosra naahin.*

*Kabira bhatti kalal ki bahu tak baithe aaey,*
*Sir saunpe soi paave, nahin tau piya na jaae.*

*Kabira rekh sindur ki aur kajal diya na jaaey,*
*Nainan preetam rum raha, duja kahan samaey.*

साधु भूखा, भाव का धन का भूखा नाहिं।
धन का भूखा जो फिरे सो तो साधू नाहिं।।

मैं लागा उस एक से एक भया सब मांहि।
सब मेरा मैं सबन का तिन्ह दूसरा नांहि।।

कबीरा भट्टी कलाल की बहु तक बैठे आय।
सिर सोंपें सोई पावैं नहीं तो पिया न जाए।।

कबीरा रेख्र सिंधूर की और काजल दिया न जाए।
नैनन प्रीतम रम रहा, दूजा कहां समाय।।

# Tulsidas
## (1532–1623)

# Tulsidas (1532–1623)

Tulsi was born at Rajapur in Banda district. His father Atma Ram Dubey was a 'prashar' brahman. His mother's name was Hulsi. As in the case of Kabir, there is uncertainty about the date of Tulsi's birth, which is variously assigned to sometime in 1554, 1585, and 1586. According to Everyman's Encyclopaedia his span of life stretched from 1532–1623, and I am inclined to accept the authenticity of these dates. It is said that he was born under a supposedly malignant star: "mool nakshatar," considered specially inauspicious for the parents. Consequently, the child Tulsi was abandoned by his parents, and forced to fend for himself. For his survival and subsistence he had to beg from door to door. It was Baba Narharidas who gave him food and shelter and saved him from the ignominy of begging. It was Narharidas again who had kindled in the heart of Tulsi the love and devotion of Ram, and had introduced him to the story of Ram's life and adventures—the story which was later to become the basis of his masterpiece: *Ram Charit Manas*. In one of his famous phrases Tulsi has paid a tacit tribute to his master, who belonged to the religious school of Swami Ramanand, the harbinger of the Bhakti movement in the North.

It is said that in his younger days, Tulsi was a very romantic and sensuous man. He was extremely fond of his wife Ratnavali to whom he was married at a young age. He couldn't bear separation from her even for a day, Ratnavali ridiculed him for his blind infatuation and exhorted him to align himself with God instead of wasting his devotion on a mere woman. Shaken out of his romantic stupor, Tulsi gave a new direction to his life and set before him the ideal of Ram worship, which became the motivating force of his life and poetry. He left his home and settled at Kashi, where he spent most of his life, reading, thinking and writing about Shri Ram. But even at Kashi he wasn't allowed to live in peace. He had to face the opposition of the local priestly clan, and had to change his habitat many a time from one spot to the other on the banks of the river Ganges. He also visited the pilgrim centres of Chitar Koot and Ayodhya. It was at Ayodhya that his great work *Ram Charit Manas* was conceived and composed. His health was frail and he fell a prey to several diseases in the later part of his life. To cure these sicknesses he could only rely on the name of God and the grace of Ram. At last he succumbed to disease and old age, and departed for his heavenly home in 1623, leaving behind him an imperishable name, and an immortal classic: *Ram Charit Manas* which is now a household word in every Hindu home, and a precious part of our national heritage. Its "dohas," "chaupaie," and "sorthas" have entered into the Hindu sub-conscious mind, and have contributed imperceptively to the moral and spiritual strenght of the common man.

Tulsi Das wrote his works in Avadhi and Brij Bhasha with equal competence, and displayed a remarkable mastery of word and phrase, of rhyme and line, and of the technicalities of the poetic art. He was a learned poet, proficient both in Hindi and Sanskrit. Although there are as many as 37 books attributed to him, the following twelve are specially noteworthy: Ram Charit Manas., Vairag Sandeepni, Ram Lalla Nachhu, Barve Ramayana, Parvati Mangal, Janki Mangal, Ramagya Prashan, Dohavali, Kavitavali, Geetavali, Krishanavli, and Vinaypatrika. His "dohas" contain a rich fund of wisdom couched in the language of the common man.

# DOHAS OF TULSIDAS

Compassion is the soul of virtue, vanity is the evil's seed,
Abandon not compassion as long as you breathe.

Treat the other's wife as mother, other's wealth as dirt,
This is the way to godliness, Tulsi Das asserts.

Greed breeds evil, anger invites death,
Compassion is the soul of religion, forgiveness, God's breath.

Self-interest is the spur behind our love and hate,
No dearth of friends for him who has wealth and state.

Where you don't get respect and are not a welcome guest,
Keep away from such a place, even if it teems in wealth.

Wealth goes to the wealthy with eager arms stretched,
But the poor, O Tulsi, are left out in the lurch.

Sons, daughters and riches may lead to evil course,
Richer far are holy meets with uplifting discourse.

*Daya dharam ka mool hai, paap mool abhiman,*
*Tulsi daya na chhorieye jab lag ghat mein praan.*

*Par dhan paththar maaniey, par istary maat samaan,*
*Itne se Hari na mile tau Tulsi Das jamaan.*

*Jahan karodh tahan kaal hai, jahan lobh tahan paap,*
*Jahan daya tahan dharm hai, jahan shama tahan aap.*

*Tulsi is sansaar mein matlib ka beopaar,*
*Jab lag paisa gaanth mein, tab lag laakhon yaar.*

*Aav nahin, aadar nahin, nahin nain mein neh,*
*Tulsi wahan na jaaieye, kanchan barse meinh.*

*Maya ko maya mile, kar kar lambe haath,*
*Tulsi Das ghareeb ki koi na poochhe baat.*

*Sut, dara, aur luxmi, paapi grah bhi hoey,*
*Sant samagham, Hari katha, Tulsi durlabh doey.*

दया धर्म का मूल है, पाप मूल अभिमान।
तुलसी दया न छोडिए, जब लग घट में प्राण।।

पर धन पत्थर मानिए, पर स्त्री मांत समान।
इतने से हरि न मिले, तो तुलसीदास जमान।।

जहां क्रोध तहां काल है, जहां लोभ तहां पाप।
जहां दया तहां धर्म है, जहां क्षमा तहां आप।।

तुलसी इस संसार में, मतलब का व्योपार।
जब तक पैसा गांठि में, तब लगि लाखों यार।।

आव नहीं आदर नहीं, नहीं नैन में नेह।
तुलसी वहां न जाइए, कंचन बरसे मेंह।।

माया को माया मिले, करि करि लम्बे हाथ।
तुलसीदास गरीब की, कोई न पूछे बात।।

सुत, दारा और लक्ष्मी, पापी गृह भी होय।
सन्त समागम हरि कथा, तुलसी दुर्लभ दोय।।

Be true in word and deed, boast not ere you achieve,
No use repenting after doing the deed.

If pride, greed, lust or rage in your heart reside,
In spite of being learned, you are yet unwise. .

If you want to test a friend, three methods apply:
Try him in need or trouble, or live as neighbour by his side.

Tulsi, living in this world, two tasks perform,
Give food to the hungry, meditate on Ram.

If you have unlimited wealth, and kingdom unconfined,
What use your wealth and might, if death haunts your mind.

Leave a dirty mind alone, lest you get besmirched,
Throw a stone in the pond, and get splashed with dirt.

Preserve a good tradition, don't break the rule,
Choose only a man of worth for love, marriage, and feud.

*Jo kahiye so kijiye, pahle kah nirdhaar,*
*Pani pi kar poochhna, kahi na bhalo vichar.*

*Kaam, karodh, moh, lobh ki jaulan man mein khan,*
*Taulon pandit, moorkhon, Tulsi ek samaan.*

*Tulsi teen parkaar se hit, unhit pahchaan,*
*Parhas pare, paros has, pare muaamla jaan.*

*Tulsi jag mein aaey ke kar lijye do kaam,*
*Dene ko tukra bhala, lene ko Hari naam,*

*Arb, kharb tak drav hai, uday ast tak raj,*
*Jo Tulsi nij maran hai, tau aawe kis kaaj.*

*Kuchh kahe neech na chheriey, bhalo na wa ko sang,*
*Paththar daare keech mein, uchhre bigare aang.*

*Tulsi kabhi na tyagieye achhe kul ki reet,*
*Laaiq ho so kijiye, beaah, ber, aur preet.*

जो कहिए सो कीजिए, पहले कह निरधार।
पानी पीकर पूछना, काहि न भलो विचार।।

काम क्रोध मद लोभ की, जौलों मन में खान।
तौलों पंडित मूरखो, तुलसी एक समान।।

तुलसी तीन प्रकार से, हित अनहित पहिचान।
पर बस पड़ पड़ोस बस, पड़े मुआमला जान।।

तुलसी जग में आये के कर लीजे दो काम।
देने को टुकड़ा भला, लेने को हरि नाम।।

अरब खरब तक द्रव्य है, उदय अस्त तक राज।
जो तुलसी निज मरन है, सो आवे किस काज।।

कुछ कहे नीच न छेड़िए, भलो न वाको संग।
पाथर डारे कीच में, उछरे बिगाड़े अंग।।

तुलसी कभी न त्यागिए, अच्छे कुल की रीत।
लायक हो सो कीजिए, व्याह, बैर और प्रीत।।

Seek knowledge from every source, be it high or low,
Even if it lies in mud, no one leaves the gold.

Those who act in thoughtless haste, sure come to grief,
It has been rightly said: Look before you leap.

A wise king, wealth and learning, a river, physician and men of class,
Where these things are wanting, shun that night resort

The sigh of a poor man carries fire untold,
Like the bellows, goat-skin made, it can melt the ore.

A word leads to many, many more succeed,
As a folded banana leaf unfolds leaf on leaf.

Greet everyone with love, treat him with warmth,
Who knows in what shape God may show His form.

He who seeks shall find, God lives inside,
The foolish world seeks Him in temples far and wide.

*Uttam vidya lijiey yadpi neech pe hoey,*
*Paro apawan thaur mein kanchan taje na koey.*

*Jo vichar bin karte hain, wah paachhe pachhtaat,*
*Taason kaaj vichaar ke, tab hi keeje baat.*

*Narip sajjan, pandit dhani, nadi vaid nij jaat,*
*Yeh japur hoen nahin, tahon na basiey raat.*

*Tulsi aah gharib hi kabhi na khali jaaey,*
*Mue bakre ki khaal se loha bhasm ho jaaey.*

*Baat baat mein baat hai,baat baat mein baat,*
*Jaise kailey ke paat mein paat paat mein paat.*

*Tulsi ya sansaar mein sab se miliey dhaaey,*
*Na jaane kis bhes mein naraayan mil jaaey.*

*Jin khoja tin paaeeya, paar braham ghat maaney,*
*Yeh jag baura ho raha, jo it ut dhoondan jaaey.*

उत्तम विद्या लीजिए, यद्यपि नीच पे होय।
पड़ो अपावन ठौर में, कंचन तजै न कोय।।

जो विचार बिन करत है, वे पाछे पछतात।
तासों काज विचार के, तब ही कीजे बात।।

नृप सज्जन पंडित धनी, नदी वैद निज जात।
यह जापुर होंय में नहीं, तहाँ न बसिए रात।।

तुलसी आह गरीब की, कभी न खाली जाय।
मुये बकरे की खाल से, लोहे भस्म हो जाय।।

बात-बात में बात है, बात बात में बात।
जैसे केले के पात में, पात पात में पात।।

तुलसी या संसार में, सबसे मिलिए धाय।
ना जाने किस भेष में, नारायण मिल जाय।।

जिन खोजा तिन पाइया, पारब्रह्म घट मांय।
यह जग बौरा हो रहा, जो इत उत ढूंढन जाय।।

Wealth is a two-legged thing, kicking from the front and hind,
Coming it makes us lose our head, going, leaves a broken mind.

How can you eat mangoes if you sow acacia seeds,
Its is a proven truth: As you sow, so shall you reap.

When you came into this world, the world smiled, you cried,
Let people cry and you smile, do such work before you die.

Store all necessary things, take my advice,
Even clay, when needed, dictates a high price.

Despite the best of company, the mean mean remains,
A snake holed in the sandal tree, stings all the same.

Do not quench your thirst, O lark, even in the lucky rain,
The thirst of love will advance your spiritual good and gain.

The tongue may wither at the root, body shrivel away,
Deeper grows the devotees' faith with every passing day.

*Daulat ki do laat hain, Tulsi nischey keen,*
*Aawat andhkaar karat hai, jaawat karmat asheen.*

*Kare buraai sukh chahe, kaise paawe koey,*
*Rope birwa aak ko, aam kahan se hoey.*

*Jab tum jag mein aaey thei, jag hansmukh tum roey,*
*Aisi karni kar chalo, tum hans mukh, jag roey.*

*Sakal vastu sangrah kare, aawe koi din kaam,*
*Waqt pare par na mile, maati kharche daam.*

*Neech nichaai nahin tajhun, sajjan hunke sang,*
*Tulsi chandan vipatbas, vish nahin tajait bhujang.*

*Chaatak, Tulsi ke mate, swaatihun piye na paani,*
*Prem trishna baarit bhali, ghate ghategi aan.*

*Ratat ratat rasna lati, trisha sookhi kai ang,*
*Tulsi chatak prem ko, nit nutan rosh rang.*

दौलत की दो लात है, तुलसी निश्चय कीन।
आवत अंधकार करत है, जावत करमत अशीन।।

करे बुराई सुख चहै, कैसे पावे कोय।
रोपे विरवा आक को, आम कहां से होय।।

जब तुम जग में आये थे, जग हंसमुख तुम रोय।
ऐसी करनी कर चलो, तुम हंसमुख जग रोय।।

सकल वस्तु संग्रह करे, आवे कोई दिन काम।
वक्त पड़े पर न मिटे, माटी खरचे दाम।।

नीच निचाई नहि तजहुं, सज्जन हूं के संग।
तुलसी चंदन विपटबसि, विष नहि तजत भुजंग।।

चातक तुलसी के मते, स्वातिंहु पिए न पानी।
प्रेम तृष्णा वाढ़ित भली, घटे घटेगी आन।।

रटत रटत रसना लटी, तृषा सूखि के अंग।
तुलसी चातक प्रेम को, नित नूतन रोष रंग।।

Ram is my sole strength, my mainstay is faith,
Lark like I always wait for the rain of His grace.

You can easily play the mentor, the disciple's role is hard indeed,
A lamb bred for yielding wool, may ruin the cotton field.

To speak and act without a thought, ignoring time and place,
Is sinning on the Ganga banks, or sighing beneath the blissful shade.

Keep away from company which may taint your mind,
A milk bottle, tavern-stacked, passes for a jug of wine.

In this world, O Tulsi, these are the gainful deeds,
Selfless service, meditation, attending spiritual meets.

Ram is a positive digit, all else is nought,
A digit multiplies to many, nought remains a nought.

Those absorbed in selfish deeds are alien to the inner peace,
Ram-devoted, selfless souls, need not fear the stings of grief,

*Ram bharoso ek bal, ek aas vishwaas,*
*Ek Ram ghansyam hit, chaatak Tulsi Das.*

*Swami hona sahaj hai, Duralbh hona daas,*
*Gaadar laye oon ko, laagi charan kapaas.*

*Desh, kaal, karta, karam, vachan vichar vihin,*
*Te surtaru tar daridi, sursari teer maleen.*

*Jeh parsang dooshan lage, tajiye tako saath,*
*Madira maanat hai jagat, doodh kalaali haath.*

*Tulsi yah sansaar mein teen vastu hain saar,*
*Ik satsang aur har bhajan, nis din par upkaar.*

*Ram Ram ko ank hai, sab saadhan hai soon,*
*Ank gaye kuchh haath nahin, ank rahe das goon.*

*Swaarth sukh sapnehun agam, parmarath na parvesh,*
*Ram Naam sumrat mithein, Tulsi kathin kalesh.*

राम भरोसो एक बल, एक आस विश्वास।
एक राम धन श्याम हित, चातक तुलसीदास।।

स्वामी होना सहज है, दुर्लभ होना दास।
गाडर लीये ऊन को, लागी चरण कपास।।

देश, काल, करता, करम, वचन विचार विहीन।
ते सुरतरू तर दारिदी, सुरसरि तीर मलीन।।

जेहि प्रसगं दूषन लगे, तजिए ताको साथ।
मदिरा मानत है जगत, दूध कलाली हाथ।।

तुलसी या संसार में, तीन वस्तु हैं सार।
इक सत्संग अरू हरिभजन, निस दिन पर उपकार।।

राम नाम को अंक है, सब साधन है सून।
अंक गए कछु हाथ नहीं, अंक रहे दस गून।।

स्वारथ सुख सपनेहूँ अगम, परमारथ न प्रवेश।
राम नाम सुमरत मिटहिं, तुलसी कठिन कलेश।।

Before I linked myself to God I was a mere reject,
Ram's name has brought me unbounded respect.

Abandon not your home or hearth, nor disrupt your family life,
With firm faith in Ram's grace, perform the daily tasks of life.

On the banks of Chitrakoot where holy saints throng,
Tulsi grinds the sandal paste, annoints the brow of Ram.

Ram worship is the gentle rain that blesses Tulsi's tree,
The twin letters "ra" and "ma" are rainy months indeed.

Pledge youself to Ram, surrender at his feet,
His grace will bless thee, give thee inner peace.

Bland are the earthly joys, Ram's name is the sweetening juice,
These words contain for sure,Tulsi, vital truth.

Repeat the sacred name of God, lose yourself in God,
All your evil inklings will at once dissolve.

*Lahin phooti kauri hoon, ko chahe, kayhi kaaj,*
*So Tulsi mahngo keo, Ram gharib niwaaz,*

*Ghar keenhein ghar jaat hai, ghar chhore ghar jaai,*
*Tulsi ghar ban beech hi, Ram prem pur chhai.*

*Chitrakoot ke ghaat par lagi santan ki bhir,*
*Tulsi Das chandan ghise, Tilak kare raghubir.*

*Varsha ritu raghupati bhagti, Tulsi saali suvaas,*
*Ram naam bar barn jug, sawan bhadon maas.*

*Ram snehi Ram gati, Ram charan rati jaahi,*
*Tulsi phal jag janam ko, deo vidhata tahi.*

*Re man sabson niras hai, saras Ram son hoh,*
*Bhali sikhawan det hai, nirdin Tulsi tohi.*

*Bigri janam anek ki sudhre abhin, aaj,*
*Hohi Ram ka naam jap, Tulsi taj kusmaaj.*

लहइन फूटी कौड़िहुं, को चाहे केहि काज।
सो तुलसी महंगो कियो, राम गरीब निवाज।।

घर कीन्हें घर जात है, घर छोड़े घर जाई।
तुलसी घर बन बीच ही, राम प्रेम पुर छाई।।

चित्रकूट के घाट पै, लगी सन्तन की भीर।
तुलसीदास चन्दन घिसें, तिलक करे रघुवीर।।

वरषारितू रघुपति भगति, तुलसी सालि सुवास।
राम नाम बर बरन जुग, सावन भादो मास।।

राम सनेही रामगति, राम चरन रति जाहि।
तुलसी फल जग जन्म को, दीयो विधाता ताही।।

रे मन सबसों निरस है, सरस राम सों होह।
भली सिखावन देत है, निरदिन तुलसी तोहि।।

बिगरी जनम अनेक की सुधरे अबहिं आज।
होहि राम का नाम जपु, तुलसी तज कुसमाज।।

Drink the nectarous grace of Ram, all desire renounce,
Like the fish submerged in water, bathe in Ram's fount.

Sweet words bring about lasting joy and peace,
If you want to win the world, abjure harsh speech.

Everyone is self-concerned, very few for others feel,
But they alone are loved and liked, who work for others' weal.

A clean-hearted man of truth, free from evil deeds,
Even in the iron age, a blissful life doth lead.

Ram's name is magic, setting rocks afloat,
Those who seek other supports are surely shallow folks.

Worship sans faith lacks force and charm,
Man remains restless without the grace of Ram.

Why express my state to Ram, omniscent, benign,
Yet self-expression gives relief, strengthens human mind.

*Sakal kamnaheen ve, Ram prem hi peen,*
*Sada charan yon rat rahe, Tulsi jeon jal meen.*

*Tulsi meethe vachan te, sukh up jat chahoon aur,*
*Vashikaran yeh mantra hai, taj de vachan kathor.*

*Aapu aapu kah sab bhalo, apne kahe koi koi,*
*Tulsi sab kah jo bhalo, sujan sarahein soi.*

*Satya vachan maanas vimal, kapt rahat kartoot,*
*Tulsi raghubar kirpa te, sake na kalyug ghoor.*

*Shri raghubir partap se, sindh tare paashaan,*
*Te mati mand jo Ram taj, bhajhim jaai prabhu aan.*

*Bin vishvaas bhagti nahin, tehi binu dravahi na Ram,*
*Ram kirpa bin sapnehoon, jeev na leh vishram.*

*Tulsi Ram kirpal son, kahi sunaoon gun dosh,*
*Hoey dubri deenta, parm peen santosh.*

सकल कामनाहीन वे, राम प्रेम ही पीन।
सदा चरन यों रत रहे, तुलसी ज्यों जल मीन।।

तुलसी मीठे वचन ते, सुख्र उपजत चहुँ ओर।
वशीकरण यह मन्त्र है, तज दे वचन कठोर।।

आपु आपु कह सब भलो, अपन कहे कोई कोई।
तुलसी सब कह जो भलो, सुजन सराहहिं सोई।।

सत्यवचन मानस विमल, कपट रहित करतूति।
तुलसी रघुवर कृपा तें सकै न कलियुग धूरि।।

श्री रघुवीर प्रताप ते, सिन्ध तरे पाषान।
ते मति मन्द जो राम तज, भजहिं जाइ प्रभु आन।।

बिनु विस्वास भगति नहीं, तेहि बिनु द्रवहि न राम।
राम कृपा बिनु सपनेहुँ, जीव न लह विश्राम।।

तुलसी राम कृपाल सों, कहि सुनाऊ गुन दोष।
होय दूबरी दीनता, परम पीन सन्तोष।।

None is happy when you prosper, the world obstructs your path,
Have faith in Ram's grace, and lo, your ship starts.

Those who wrap themselves in rags, skull in hand parade,
Masquerade as holy men in the iron age.

Those who covet others' wealth, lust for others' wives,
Are the devil's offspring, in human form disguised.

Ram discourse is the cow, soul-suffusing is her milk,
Saintly meets are visions of heaven, all the wise admit.

Mind is the ploughman, body is the field,
Good and evil are the seeds, as you sow, you reap.

Eternal is the grace of Ram, his merits unconfined,
They take it for the gospel truth, the pure, enlightened minds.

Merit brings name and fame, no merit, no fame,
People love a warbling bird, a crow croaks in vain.

*Badhak sab sabke bhaye, sadhak bhayo na koi,*
*Tulsi Ram kirpalu te, bhali hoi so hoi.*

*Ashubh bhesh bhushan dhare, bhashya bhashya je khahein,*
*Tei yogi tei sidh nar, poojyate kalyug maanhein.*

*Pardrohi pardaar rat, par dhan par apwad,*
*Te nar paamar paap maye, deh dhare manujaad.*

*Ram katha surdhenu sam, sewat sab sukhdan,*
*Sant sabha surlok sam, ko na sune asjaan.*

*Tulsi kaya khet hai, mansa bhaye kisaan,*
*Paap pun do beej hain, boey so le nidaan.*

*Ram anant anant gun, amit katha vistaar,*
*Suni ashcharya na maanihahim, jinke vimal vichaar.*

*Maan hot hai gunan se, gun bin maan na hoey,*
*Shukra saari raakhe sabhi, kaag na raakhe koey.*

बाधक सब सबके भये, साधक भयो न कोई।
तुलसी राम कृपालु ते, भली होइ सो होइ।।

अशुभ वेष भूषण धरे, भक्ष्याभक्ष्य जे खाहिं।
तेइ योगी तेइ सिद्ध नर, पूज्यते कलयुग माहिं।।

परद्रोही परदार रत, पर धन पर अपवाद।
ते नर पामर पापमय, देह धरे मनुजाद।।

रामकथा सुरधेनु सम, सेवत सब सुखदानि।
संत सभा सुरलोक सम, को न सुने असजानि।।

तुलसी काया खेत है, मनसा भये किसान।
पाप पुण्य दो बीज हैं, बोये सो ले निदान।।

राम अनन्त अनन्त गुण, अमित कथा विस्तार।
सुनि आश्चर्य न मानिहहिं, जिनके विमल विचार।।

मान होत है गुनन से, गुन बिन मान न होय।
शुक्र सारी राखे सभी, काग न राखे कोय।।

As the eye collyrium-touched awakens to the surrounding sights,
So a man of inner vision sees the Lord actualized.

Shut your eyes and ears and mouth, concentrate on God,
The inner window opens when outer doors are barred.

The attempt to reach the glorious heights without Ram's gracious prop,
Is the attempt to scale the skies, holding on to a rain-drop.

Desire is the deity strange among the several gods,
Transcend desire, feel at peace, worship her and kiss the rod.

Soldiers, saints, scholars, men of virtuous deeds,
Lose their magic power, if tainted with greed.

The rain with its gentle hug cools the earth's crust,
Don't blame the water if you are still athirst.

Recite the sacred name of Ram with heart, soul, and lip,
Be it youth, age, or end, Ram will guide your ship.

*Yatha suanjan aanji hug, saadhak, sidh sujaan,*
*Kautuk dekhi shailwan, bhootal bhoori nidhaan.*

*Aankh, kaan, mukh moond ke, naam niranjan le,*
*Bhitar ke pat tab khule,jab baahar ke pat de.*

*Ram naam avlambhbinu, parmarath ko aas,*
*Barsat varidhi boond gahi, chahat charhan akaas.*

*Tulsi adbhut devta, aasa devi naam,*
*Sewe seek samarpeye, vimukh bhaye abhiram.*

*Giani, taapas, sur, kavi, kovid guni aagaar,*
*Kaihi ke lobh vidambna, kahin ahi sansaar.*

*Barkhi wishv harshit karat, harat taap, adhpyaas,*
*Tulsi dosh na jalaj ko, jo jal jal jare jawaas.*

*Preet, pratit, surin son, Ram naam jap Ram,*
*Tulsi tera hai bhala, aadi, madhya, awsaan.*

यथा सुअञ्जन आँजि हग, साधक सिद्ध सुजान।
कौतुक देखहि शैलवन, भूतल भूरि निधान।।

आंख कान मुख मूंद के, नाम निरंजन ले।
भीतर के पट तब खुले, जब बाहर के पट दे।।

राम नाम अवलम्बबिनु, परमारथ को आस।
बरसत वारिधि बून्द गहि, चाहत चढ़न अकास।।

तुलसी अद्‌भुत देवता, आसा देवी नाम।
सेवे सीक समरपिह, विमुख भये अभिराम।।

ज्ञानी, तापस सूर कवि, कोविद गुनी आगार।
केहि के लोभ विडम्बना, केहिन एहि संसार।।

बरखि विरव हरषित करत, हरत ताप अधप्यास।
तुलसी दोष न जलज को, जो जल जल जरै जवास।।

प्रीत प्रतीत सुरीन सों, रामनाम जप राम।
तुलसी तेरो है भला, आदि मध्य अवसान।।

What ever I am, good or bad, I am yours complete,
Nowhere can I find refuge except at your feet.

Temptation rides rough-shod on earth, armed from hilt to heel,
With greed, lust and fraud equipped, it swoops over the field.

Those who worship without a cause, unthinking upbraid,
Such men are the purblind bats, be not by them swayed.

The whole world is self-obsessed, unconcerned with public weal,
Be thou wise and selfless, worship Ram with zeal.

Those who venerate their parents, hold their teacher in respect,
Blissful is their course of life, free from all regret.

Love, service, and charity, confidence, self-respect,
These five virtues make a man perfect.

Devotion to the name of Ram ensures joy and peace,
The sluggard neglecting Ram naam life-in-death doth lead.

*Jaise taise raavro, kewal kaushal pal,*
*To Tulsi ko hai bhalo, tihun lok tihun kaal.*

*Vyapi rahe sansaar manhun, maya kapat prachand,*
*Senapati kaamadi bhat, dambh kapat, paakhand.*

*Bhalo kahhin binu jahu, bine jaane apwaad,*
*Te chamgadur jaani jiye, kari man harsh vishaad.*

*Mor mor sab kah kahih, tu tau kah nij naam,*
*Kay chup saadh sun samujh hain, Tulsi japu Ram.*

*Maatra, pita, guru, swami sikh, sir dhari karhin subhaye,*
*Laheu labhu tin janam kar, natru janam jag jaaye.*

*Punya, preet, pati,prasamtiu, parmarath path paanch,*
*Lahih sujan pariharhi khall, sunhou sikhawan saanch.*

*Ram naam japi jo jan, bhaye sukrit sukhshal,*
*Tulsi jahan jo aalsi, gayo aaju kokaal.*

जैसे तैसे रावरो, केवल कौशल पाल।
तो तुलसी को है भलो, तिहुँ लोकतिहूँ काल।।

व्यापि रहेउ संसार महुँ माया कपट प्रचण्ड।
सेनापति कामादि भट, दम्भ कपट पाखंड।।

भलो कहहिं बिनु जनेहु, बिन जाने अपवाद।
ते चमगादुर जानि जिये, करि मन हरष विषाद।।

मोर मोर सब कह कहहि, तू तो कह निज नाम।
कै चुप साधहि सुन समुझ हैं तुलसी जपु राम।।

मातु पिता गुरु स्वामि सिख्, सिर धरि करहिं सुभाय।
लहेउ लाभु तिहं जनम कर, नतरू जन्म जग़ जाय।।

पुन्य प्रीति पति प्रस्मतिउ, परमारथ पथ पांच।
लहहि सुजन परिहरहि खल, सुनहु सिखावन सांच।।

राम नाम जपि जोहजन, भये सुकृत सुखशालि।
तुलसी जहां जो आलसी, गयो आजु कोकालि।।

The nameless Being, beyond our ken, eternal, unperceived,
That Supreme directs the show, creates the world we see.

Those who want to rise in life by pulling down their mates,
Are sure to fall in the public eye, earn perpetual hate.

Those who meditate on Ram luxuriate in bliss,
Sinful sluggards, forgetting Ram, life's purpose miss.

The city resounds with pipes and drums, a festive mood prevails,
People sing and dance with joy, and little Ram his antics plays.

Tempting are the snares of life, puzzling are its ways,
Seek refuge in Rama's name if you would be saved.

Everyone in Ram Rajya did righteous course pursue,
Vice and sin took to their heels, love and peace did rule.

Garden-like the body blooms, the mind fragrance blows,
Eyes fertilize the fields, when Ram grace bestows.

*Gian gira gotit aj, maya gun gopaar,*
*Soi sachidanand dhan, karat charitra udaar.*

*Tulsi je kirati chahhin, parhar kirat khoi,*
*Tinke munh masi lagi, hain mithin mir hai dhoi.*

*Ram (naam) gharib niwaaz ko, rajdet janjaan,*
*Tulsi man parihar tinhi raghubani, chaki baani.*

*Anudit awadh bandhawte, nit nav manglamod,*
*Mudit maatrapitra log lakhi, rahubar baal vinod.*

*Hari maya krit dosh gun, binu hari bhajan na jaahein,*
*Bhajiye Ram sab kaam taji, as vichaar man maanhin.*

*Ram raj rajat sakal, dharm nirat narnaari,*
*Raag, na rosh, na dosh dukh, sulabh adarath chaari.*

*Pulak vatika, bagh ban, sukh suvihang-biharu,*
*Mali suman sneh jal, seenchat lochan chaaru.*

ज्ञान-गिरा गोतीत अज, माया गुन गोपार।
सोइ सच्चिदानन्द धन, करत चरित्र उदार।।

तुलसी जे कीरति चहहिं, परहर कीरत खोइ।
तिनके मुंह मसि लागि हैं, मिटहिंन मीर है धोइ।।

राम (नाम) गरीब निवाज को, राजदेत जन जानि।
तुलसी मन परिहर तिनहि रघुबनि चाकी बानि।।

अनुदित अवध बंधावते, नित नव मंगलामोद।
मुदित मातु पितु लोग लखि, रघुवर बालविनोद।।

हरि माया कृत दोष गुन, बिनु हरि भजन न जाहिं।
भजिय राम सब काम तजि, अस विचार मन माहिं।।

राम-राज राजत सकल, धरम निरत नरनारि।
राग न रोष न दोष दुःख, सुलभ पदारथ चारि।।

पुलक वाटिका बाग बन, सुख सुविहंग-बिहारु।
माली सुमन सनेह जल, सींचत लोचन चारु।।

Folks neglecting salvation, waste away their lives,
The fools finding fault with God are virtual suicides.

A crane can't become a swan, if it apes his garb and gait,
If we sift milk from water, the crane stands betrayed.

What in Satyug, Doapar Treta, yagya, yog, and prayer achieve,
Recitation of Ram Naam in the iron age doth yield.

Ram naam is going cheap, grab it quick and fast,
You'll make vain regrets, when death blows its blast.

Truth is the highest virtue, falsehood, the greatest fault,
He who has truth at heart, is the very spirit of God.

He who helps the helpless with selfish gain in view,
Avoid even his ugly sight, he is a sinner through and through.

The world consists, Tulsi, of diverse kinds of folk,
Greet them all with a smile, it's a gathering in a boat.

*Jo na tare bhawsagarhi, nar samaan aspaye,*
*So krit nindak mandmati, aatamhan gati jaaye.*

*Charan chonch lochan rangon, chalo maraali chaal,*
*Chheer neer virchan samay, bak uchhrat tihi kaal.*

*Satyug, treta, doapar, pooja, makh aruyog,*
*Jo gati hoe so kalihhari naamtepal hi log.*

*Loot sake tau loot le. Ram Naam ki loot,*
*Paachhe phir pachhtaoge, pran jahin jab chhoot.*

*Saanch barabar tap nahin,jhoot barabar paap,*
*Jake hirday saanch hai, taake hirday aap.*

*Sarnagat kahi jate jahin nij anihit anuman,*
*Te nar paamar paapmay, tihhin bilokat han.*

*Tulsi is sansaar mein, bhaanti bhaanti ke log,*
*Sab se has mil boliye, nadi naav sanjog.*

जो न तरै भवसागरहि, नर समान असपाय।
सो कृत निन्दक मंदमति, आतमहन गति जाय।।

चरन चोंच लोचन रंगों, चलो मराली चाल।
छीर नीर विरचन समय, बक उछरत तिहि काल।।

सतयुग, त्रेता, द्वापर, पूजा मख्र अरू योग।
जो गति होय सो कलिहहरि नामतेपाल हि लोग।।

लूट सकै तो लूट लै, राम-नाम की लूट।
पाछे फिरि पछताऔगे, प्राण जाहिं जब छूट।।

साँच बराबर तप नहीं, झूठ बराबर पाप।
जाके हिरदे साँच है, ताके हिरदे आप।।

सरनागत कहि जते जहिं, निज अनिहित अनुमानि।
ते नर पामर पापमय, तिहहिं बिलोकत हानि।।

तुलसी इस संसार में, भाँति भाँति के लोग।
सबसे हस मिल बोलिए, नदी नाव संजोग।।

# Rahim

(1556–1627)

# Rahim (1556–1627)

Abdur Rahim Khankhana was a man of versatile talent — a poet, a soldier, a statesmen, and a scholar, endowed with a catholicity of outlook which made no distinction between mosque or shrine, race or religion. He was born at Lahore on December 17, 1556, the year of Humayun's death. His father, Bairam Khan, was a chieftain of Badakhshan (Turkistan) and a trusted lieutenant of Humayun. It was Bairam Khan who had helped Humayun in re-capturing the throne of Delhi for the second time in 1555. It was Bairam Khan again who, after the death of Humayun in 1556, had installed Akbar as the king of Delhi, and helped him in the difficult task of governance. But due to personal jealousy, and the fear of his rising popularity, Akbar fell foul of Bairam Khan, and ordered him to go on exile for a pilgrimage to Mecca. He was assaulted on the way and treacherously murdered by an Afghan, Mubarak Khan. Bairam Khan was married to the younger sister of Humayun's wife, and was thus closely linked with the royal family. Because of his proximity to the royal household, the task of the education and upbringing of his son, Abdur Rahim, (who was only four years old when his father died) was undertaken by Akbar himself. It must have been during this period at Agra that Rahim acquired proficiency in several languages — Turkish, Persian, Arabic, Sanskrit and Hindi. He was married at a young age to a girl of the royal family, Mah Bano, and became, like his father, a relation of the king. Later, his daughter was married to prince Daniyal, and his grand daughter to Shahjehan. By the age of 19, Rahim was already an accomplished general, who had successfully quelled a dangerous uprising in Gujrat. Later, he won many successes in his expeditions in the South, and was instrumental in extending and consolidating the empire of Akbar.

He was consequently loaded with wealth and honour. But kingly favours are fickle and unpredictable, suddenly granted, and as suddenly withdrawn. In the time of Jehangir, the successor of Akbar, he fell a prey to the jealousy of the king's two sons, Parvez and Murad, who treated him with slight and disrespect. As he advanced in years he had to suffer the blows of chance and fate. He saw the death of his wife, the deaths of his two sons and sons-in-law, and the tragic loss of his grandsons. As if this was not enough, one of his sons was beheaded, and his severed head was offered to him in a plate, saying that it contained the gift of a water-melon. Rahim accepted the cruel joke stoically, calling it a 'martyred melon." Furthermore, he had to suffer incarceration in jail, from which he was released a year before his death, that came in 1627, when he was nearly 72.

In his figure and features Rahim was a handsome youth. He is generally shown as a smart and stout young man, wearing on his head an impressive turban with ornamental folds, his left hand clutching a bejewelled sword, his right hand stretched for friendship, or for doling out charity. He was very generous but very modest, and never bragged about his philanthropy. His attitude is neatly reflected in the following verse:

*It is God who giveth us, unasked, unsought,*

*We feel embarrassed when thanked for naught.*

In the words of Keshavdas, Rahim was like the arrows of Shri Rama, out to destroy the wicked, and defend the weak and the innocent. He was also a man of high moral calibre. Once he was solicited by a young girl, who wanted him to give her a son of his loins. Throwing his head in the lap of the girl, he said : "Treat me as your son, for who knows what kind of a child, if at all, is born out of our union."

Rahim had started writing poetry at the age of eleven. He was influenced primarily by the writings of Kalidas, Surdas, and Tulsi. Rahim and Tulsi (1532-1623) were, infact, contemporaries, and both of them have benefited from each other's literary merits. Both of them were also important poets of the Bhakti movement which was aimed at reviving the essential spirit of religion, purged of hollow ritual and divisive dogma.

Having lived at Delhi and Agra Rahim had acquired a thorough mastery of Braj Bhasha which is the basic language of his "dohas."

At the same time he had imbibed, since childhood, the grace and grandeur of Persian poetry, and this double competence in Persian and Hindi has lent the characteristics of softness and strength to his poetic style. He had also translated *Tazkara-e-Babri* from Turkish into Persian language, which had brought him great fame in the literary circles. It is remarkable that though he spent his life with kings and courtiers, he wrote for the common reader, who loves him for the simplicity and clarity of his thought and style. Having seen the ups and downs of life, Rahim had acquired deep understanding of human nature and a fine sense of discrimination. Sensitivity to honour and self-respect, value of love and friendship, distrust of kings and courtiers, faith in the sovereignty of time and fate, admiration for a life of contentment and self-discipline, and, above all, devotion to Lord Krishna — a quality which aligns him with Surdas — are some of the recurring themes of his "dohas."

# DOHAS OF RAHIM KHANKHANA

# DOHAS OF RAHIM KHANKHANA

Bear up with the evil days, don't grumble or bewail,
Things will straighten out themselves, let better times prevail.

We are in a sorry pass, know not what to do,
God forbids falsehood, the world dislikes truth.

Snakes, steeds, guns and women, kings, men of lower breed,
Can recoil anytime, beware Rahiman, take heed.

Useless are its blooms and branches, fruits as well as leaves,
Yet it blocks the traveller's path, the wild, acacia tree.

Currying favour with the rich undermines your self-respect,
Which you can't retrieve by spending all your wealth.

By pleasing the One you please so many, by pleasing many none at all,
If you care to tend the roots, fruits and flowers will come unasked.

No dearth of sychophants when you have wealth and ease,
You can know the false from true only at the time of need.

*Ab Rahim chup kari rahu, samujh dinan ka pher,*
*Jab din neeke aai hai, banat na lagi hai der.*

*Ab Rahim mushkil pari, garhe do-oo kaam*
*Saanche se tau jag nahin, jhute mile na Ram*

*Urg, turang, naari, narpati, neech jaati, hathyaar,*
*Rahimin inhein sambhareye, paltat lage na baar.*

*Aap na kaahu kaam ke, daar paat phalphool,*
*Auran ko rokatphiren, Rahman per babool.*

*Aadar ghate nares dhig, basi rahe kachhu naahin,*
*Jo Rahim kotin mile, dhig jeevan jag maahein*

*Eke saadhe sab sadhe, sab saadhe, sab jaaye,*
*Rahiman moolh seenchibo, phoole phale aghaey.*

*Kahe Rahim sampati sage, banat bahut bahut reet,*
*Vipati kasauti je kase, te hi saanche meet.*

# अब्दुल रहीम खानखाना

अब रहीम चुप करि रहउ, समुझ दिनन का फेर।
जब दिन नीके आई है, बनत न लगि है देर।।

अब रहीम मुश्किल पड़ी, गाढ़े दोऊ काम।
सांचे से तो जग नहीं, झूठे मिले न राम।।

उरग, तुरंग, नारी, नृपति, नीच जाति, हथियार।
रहिमन इन्हें संभारिए, पलटत लगे न बार।।

आप न काहू काम के, डार पात फल फूल।
औरन को रोकत फिरैं, रहिमन पेड़ बबूल।।

आदर घटे नरेस धिग, बसे रहे कछु नाहिं।
जो रहीम कोटिन मिले, धिग जीवन जग माहिं।।

एकै साधे सब सधै, सब साधै सब जाय।
रहिमन मूलहिं सींचिबो, फूलै फलै अघाय।।

कहि रहीम संपति सगे, बनत बहुत बहुत रीत।
विपति कसौटी जे कसे, ते ही सांचे मीत।।

How much of your life is gone, how little is left,
In lusts and greeds you spent your days, now you make regrets.

Fickle is the goddess of wealth, all the world doth know,
The bride of an old man, some restlessness must show.

A hawk with a broken wing is like a broken weed,
Yet the Creator feeds him, caters to his need.

What use is paradise and the wishful filling tree?
Better lie beneath the "dhak", beside your darling sweet.

How can to the rich and high the poor turn hostile,
A fish dwelling in the sea can't offend the crocodile.

Expenses rise, means decline, the king gives no aid,
Like a fish in shallow waters, man lives dismayed.

Chop off the cucumber's head, rub it hard with salt,
This is the proper cure of the folks bitter at heart.

*Kahu Rahim ketik rahi, ketik gai bihaye,*
*Maya mamta moh pari, ant chale pachhtaye.*

*Kamla thir na Rahim kahi, yeh jaanat sab koey,*
*Pursh puraatam ki badhu, kyon na chanchal hoey.*

*Kaam na kahu aawai, mol Rahim na laee,*
*Baaj toote baaj ko, sahib chara deyi.*

*Kaah karoon baikunth let kalp bariksh ki chhaan,*
*Rahiman daakh suhawno, jo gal peetam baanh.*

*Kaise nibhein nibal jan, kar sablan son gair,*
*Rahiman bas sagar vishe, karat magar son ber.*

*Kharch barheo, udham ghateo, narpati nithur man keen,*
*Kaho Rahim kaise jieye, thore jal ki meen.*

*Khira sir se kaateye, maliat namak lagaey*
*Rahmin karuey mukhan ko chahat ihi sajaaey.*

कहू रहीम केतिक रही, केतिक गई बिहाय।
माया ममता मोह परि, अंत चले पछिताय।।

कमला थिर न रहीम कहि, यह जानत सब कोय।
पुरुष पुरातन की बधू, क्यों न चंचला होय।।

काम न काहू आवई, मोल रहीम न लेई।
बाज टूटे बाजे को, साहब चारा देई।।

काह करौं बैकुंठ लै, कलप बृच्छ की छाँह।
रहिमन दाख सुहावनो, जो गल पीतम बाँह।।

कैसे निबहैं निबल जन, कर सबलन सों गैर।
रहिमन बस सागर विषे, करत मगर सों बैर।।

रवरच बढ़यो, उद्यम घट्यो, नृपति निठुर मन कीन।
कहु रहीम कैसे जिये, थोरे जल की मीन।।

खीरा सिर ते काटिए, मलियत नमक लगाए।
रहिमन करूए मुखन को, चहिअत इहै सज़ाय।।

Murder, scent, cough and hatred, joy, drink, romance,
Cannot be concealed for long , knoweth every man.

Food is dear to us all, it can pep up fainting hearts,
As we rub the dough on drum, it begins to thrum and throb.

Eschew desire, conquer care, set your mind at ease,
If you are desire-free, you are a king indeed.

Rahiman, Ram, the king of Awadh, at Chitrakoot resides,
When men in distress need him, his grace at once arrives.

Those who love and kiss the poor deserve the highest praise,
Remember how Sudama poor was by Krishan embraced!

The great owe their strength to the small,Rahiman thus opines,
A penny-worth of nails, a thousand things can bind.

So long as there is life, joy and sorrow assert their might,
When the chess pawn is killed, they too vanish from the sight.

*Khair, khoon, khansi, khusi, ber, preeti, madpaan,*
*Rahiman daabe na dabe, jaanat sakal jahaan.*

*Chara payara jagat mein, chhala hit kar lay,*
*Jeon Rahim aata lage, teon mirdang swar dey.*

*Chah gai, chinta miti, manuaa beparwah,*
*Jinko kuchh na chaaheye, wah sahab ke saah.*

*Chitrakoot mein rami rahe, Rahiman awadh-nares,*
*Ja par bipda parat hai, to aawat yehi des.*

*Je ghareeb par hit kare, te Rahim bar log,*
*Kahan Sudama baapuro, Krishan mitaai jog.*

*Chhoten so sohain bare, kahe Rahim eh rekh,*
*Sahsan ko hai baandhiat, le damri ki mekh.*

*Jab lag jeevan jagat mein, sukh dukh milan agot,*
*Rahiman phoote got jeon, parat duhan sir chot.*

खैर, खून, खांसी, खुसी, बैर प्रीति मदपान।
रहिमन दाबे न दबैं, जानत सकल जहान।।

चारा प्यारा जगत में, छाला हित कर लेय।
जयों रहीम आटा लगे, त्यों मृदंग स्वर देय।।

चाह गई चिन्ता मिटी, मनुआ बेपरवाह।
जिनकों कुछ न चाहिए, वे साहब के साह।।

चित्रकूट में रमि रहे, रहिमन अवध-नरेस।
जा पर विपदा पड़त है, तो आवत यहि देस।।

जे गरीब पर हित करैं, ते रहीम बड़ लोग।
कहां सुदामा बापुरो, कृष्ण मिताई जोग।।

छोटेन सो सोहैं, बड़े, कहि रहीम यह रेख।
सहसन को हम बांधियत, लै दमरी की मेख।।

जब लगि जीवन जगत में, सुख दुख मिलन अगोट।
रहिमन फूटे गोट ज्यों, परत दुहन सिर चोट।।

If you are devoid of means, you are shunned by one and all,
Even he sun turns hostile to a lotus water-starved.

By our own acts controlled, puppet-like we rock and roll,
Our own handiwork, Rahim, lo, rejects our own control.

The smouldering fire finally dies, once dead, it can't revive,
The fire of love remains alive, snuff it as much as you like.

He who inheres our being, and in our heart resides.
Needn't be in terms explicit, of our sorry state apprised.

It's our faulty sense that our speech prescribes,
Bear with a stupid man, he can't change his style.

Our body has to put up with whatever be the state,
Be it rain, shine, or snow, the earth bears the weight.

Bad company can't corrupt a pure and noble mind,
The sandal tree remains untainted, even if' snake-entwined.

*Jab lagi bin na aapune, tab lag mitra na koey,*
*Rahiman ambuj ambu bin, ravi nahin hit hoey.*

*Jeon naachat kathputri, karam nachavat gaat,*
*Apne haath Rahim jeon, nahin aapune haath.*

*Je sulge te bujh gaye, bujhe te sulge naahin,*
*Rahiman daahe prem ke, bujh bujh ke sulgaahin.*

*Jehi Rahim tan man leo, kyon hiey bich bhaun,*
*Taason sukh dukh kahan ki, rahi baat ab kaun.*

*Jaisi jaaki budhi hai, taisi kahe banaey,*
*Toko bura na maaneye, len kahan so jaaey.*

*Jaisi pare so sahi rahe, kahi Rahim yeh deh,*
*Dharti par hi parat hai, sheet, dhaam aur meinh.*

*Jo Rahim uttam prakriti, ka kasi sakal kusang,*
*Chandan vish vayapat nahin, lapte rahat bhujang.*

जब लग बित्त न आपुने, तब लग मित्र न कोय।
रहिमन अंबुज अमबु बिन, रवि नहीं हित होय।।

ज्यों नाचत कठपूतरी, करम नचावत गात।
अपने हाथ रहीम ज्यों, नहीं आपुने हाथ।

जे सुलगे ते बुझ गये, बुझे ते सुलगे नाहिं।
रहिमन दाहे प्रेम के, बुझ बुझ के सुलगाहिं।।

जेहि रहीम तन मन लियो, कियो हिये बिच भौन।
तासों सुख दुख कहन की, रही बात अब कौन।।

जैसी जाकी बुद्धि है, तैसी कहे बनाय।
ताकों बुरा न मानिये, लेन कहां सो जाए।।

जैसी परै सो सहि रहै, कहि रहीम यह देह।
धरती पर ही परत है, शीत, धाम और मेह।।

जो रहीम उत्तम प्रकृति, का करि सकल कुसंग।
चंदन विष व्यापत नहीं, लपटे रहत भुजंग।।

A lowly man when upraised, false airs displays,
A pawn promoted as a bishop, acquires a slanting gait.

A faithful son, O Rahim, is like a lamp at night,
All is dark where he is not, with him all is bright.

What the saintly souls reject, the silly folks embace,
The dog eats with relish, what humans evacuate.

With our own hands we do what our fate dictates,
Ravana couldn't have kidnapped Sita but for Ram's deer-chase.

You should do your very best to conciliate the parted mates,
As we re-arrange the beads which have got displaced.

The river doesn't drink its water, the tree doesn't eat its fruit,
The good and wise spend their wealth for the public use.

Moderate means but high respect, this should be our goal,
The bride of a noble home feels content with tattered clothes.

*Jo Rahim ochho barhe, tau ati hi itraey,*
*Pyadey se farzi bhayo, terho terho jaae.*

*Jo Rahim gati deep ki, sut sapoot ki soey,*
*Bare ujero lage, bare andhero hoey.*

*Jo vishya artan taji, moorh tahi laptaey,*
*Jeon nar darat baman kar, swaan swaad son khaaey.*

*Jo Rahim bhavi katon, hoti aapune haath,*
*Ram na jaate hiran sang, siay na Ravan saath.*

*Toote sujan manaaiye, jo toote sau baar,*
*Rahiman phiri phir poheye, toote muktahaar.*

*Taruvar phal nahin khaat hai, sarvar piyahin na paan,*
*Kahi Rahim kar kaaj hit, sampati sanchahi sujaan.*

*Dhan thoro izzat bari, kah Rahim ka baat,*
*Jaise kul ki kulbadhu, chithran manh samaat.*

जो रहीम ओछो बढ़ै, तो अति ही इतराय।
प्यादे से फरजी भयो, टेढ़ो टेढ़ो जाय।।

जो रहीम गति दीप की, सुत सपूत की सोय।
बारे उजियारो लगे, बढ़े अंधेरो होय।।

जो विषया संतन तजी, मूढ़ ताहि लपटाय।
ज्यों नर डारत वमन कर, स्वाद स्वाद सों खाय।।

जो रहीम भावी कतौं, होति आपुने हाथ।
राम न जाते हरिन संग, सीय न रावन साथ।।

टूटे सुजन मनाइए, जौ टूटे सौ बार।
रहिमन फिरि फिरि पोहिए, टूटे मुक्ताहार।।

तरुवर फल नहिं खात है, सरवर पियहिं न पान।
कहि रहीम पर काज हित, संपति संचहि सुजान।।

धन थोरो इज़्ज़त बड़ी, कह रहीम का बात।
जैसे कुल की कुलबधू, चिथड़न मांह समात।।

The earth bears with every state, heat, cold, or rain,
So doth our body bear, sweet and sour, joy and pain.

Action lies in our hand, the fruit rests with Fate,
We can only throw the dice, and not predict its shape.

Seeing the heavy rains arrive, the koel sits mum and mute,
In the din of coaking frogs, who will hear her lute?

When our love fills our eyes, nothing else attracts our sight,
The traveller returns from the door seeing the house is occupied.

Love is not a child's play, but a deadly serious game,
It's to ride a horse of wax, and push into the fiery main.

The great hate self-praise, hollow boast despise,
Does the diamond ever say: millions is my price?

It's hard to set straight the things once embroiled,
Curdled milk yields no butter, you may sweat ad toil.

*Dharti ki so reet hai, seet, ghaam aur meinh,*
*Jaisi pare so sahi rahe, teon Rahim yeh deh.*

*Nij kar kria Rahim kah, sudhi bhavi ke haath,*
*Paanse apne haath mein, daanw na apne haath.*

*Paawas dekhi Rahim man, koel saadhe maun,*
*Ab dadur bakta bhaye, humko poochhat kaun.*

*Preetam chhabi nainan basi, par chhabi kahan samaaey,*
*Bhari sarai Rahim lakhi, pathak aap phir jaaey.*

*Prem panth aiso kathin, sab kou nibhat naahin,*
*Rahiman main-turang chahi,chaleo pawak maahin.*

*Bare baraai na karen, baro na bolen bol,*
*Rahiman hira kab kahe, laakh taka mero mol.*

*Bigri baat baney nahin, laakh karo kin koey,*
*Rahiman phaate doodh ko, mathe na makhan hoey.*

धरती की सो रीत है, सीत, धाम और मेह।
जैसी परे सो सहि रहे, त्यों रहीम यह देह।।

निज कर क्रिया रहीम कह, सुधि भावी के हाथ।
पांसे अपने हाथ में, दांव न अपने हाथ।।

पावस देखि रहीम मन, कोइल साधे मौन।
अब दादुर वक्ता भये, हमको पूछत कौन।।

प्रीतम छबि नैनन बसी, पर छवि कहां समाय।
भरी सराय रहीम लखि, पाथक आप फिर जायं।।

प्रेम पंथ एसो कठिन, सब कोउ निबहत नाहिं।
रहिमन मैन-तुरंग चढ़ि, चलिबो पावक माहिं।।

बड़े बड़ाई ना करैं, बड़ों न बोलैं बोल।
रहिमन हीरा कब कहै, लाख टका मेरो मोल।।

बिगरी बात बनै नहीं, लाख करौ किन कोय।
रहिमन फाटे दूध को, मथे न माखन होय।।

Stores of wealth help thee not in times adverse,
Seeing the dawn arrive, the million stars disperse.

Butter doesn't change with churning, curd and whey split,
A true friend, whatever befalls, never gives a slip.

The fish, when chopped, is washed in water, when eaten, kindles thirst,
Marvellous is the force of love, steadfast in the face of death.

None, Rahim, is born a master, bear this truth in mind,
Love, hate, honour and talent, ripen with the time.

Narrow is the lane of love, allowing only one to pass,
If 'I' lives, God departs, when God arrives, "I" dissolves.

The great and good behave, Rahim, like a faithful steed,
Which saves the rider from the harm, even if it trips and bleeds.

A stupid man is the source of pain both in love and hate,
Whether a dog bites or licks, it helps us neither way.

*Bipati bhaye dhan ana rahe, rahe jo laakh karor,*
*Nabh taare chhip jaat hain, jeon Rahim bhaye bhor.*

*Mathan mathan maakhan rahe, dahi mahi bilgaaey,*
*Rahiman soi meet hai, bhir pare thahraaey.*

*Meen kati jal dhoieye, khaaey adhik payaas,*
*Rahiman preet saraheye, mucheu meet ke aas.*

*Yeh Rahim nij sang le, janmat jagat na koey,*
*Ber, preet, abhyass, jas, hot hot ho jaeye.*

*Rahiman gali hai saankri, doojo na thahrahin,*
*Aapu ahai tau hari nahin, hari tau aapun naahin.*

*Yon Rahim gati baren ki, tayon turang vayovhar,*
*Daagh diwawat aapu tan, sahi hot aswaar.*

*Rahiman ochh narn son, ber bhale na preet,*
*Kaate chaate swaan ke, do-oo bhanti vipreet.*

विपति भए धन न रहे, रहे जो लाख करोर।
नभ तारे छिप जात हैं, ज्यों रहीम भय भोर।।

मथन मथन माखन रहै, दही मही बिलगाय।
रहिमन सोई मीत है, भीर परे ठहराय।।

मीन कटि जल धोइये, खाय अधिक पियास।
रहिमन प्रीति सराहिये, मुचेउ मीत कै आस।।

यह रहीम निज संग लै, जनमत जगत न कोय।
बैर, प्रीति, अभ्यास, जस, होत होत हो जाय।।

रहिमन गली है सांकरी, दूजो ना ठहराहिं।
आपु अहै तो हरि नहीं, हरि तो आपुन नाहिं।।

यों रहीम गति बड़ेन की, त्यों तुरंग व्यवहार।
दाग दिवावत आपु तन, सही होत असवार।।

रहिमन ओछ नरन सों, बैर भले न प्रीति।
काटे चाटै स्वान के, दोऊ भाँति विपरीति।।

Man can survive the wound by bow and arrow caused,
Fatal is the dart, Rahim, by the arched eyes discharged.

Small men can't perform big and weighty tasks,
The hide of a hundred rats can't cover the timbre top.

The crazy tongue wags and wags, without a pause or thought,
Having wagged, it slinks back, the skull reaps the wrath.

When you sight the bigger thing, discard not the small,
What a needle does for you, the sword can't at all.

Why expose your heart and soul to one and all in vain,
People hear but cannot share your inner grief and pain.

Don't snap the thread of love in an angry fit,
Once snapped it can't rejoin without a knot betwixt.

Nothing but your own resource can serve your urgent need,
The sun alone can't revive a water-famished lotus reed.

*Rahiman teer ki chot te, chot pare bach jaaey,*
*Nain baan ki chot se, chot pare mari jaaey.*

*Rahiman chhote naran son, hot baro nahin kaam,*
*Marho damamo na baney, sau choohe ke chaam.*

*Rahiman jibha bawri, kah gai sarag pataal,*
*Aapu tau kahi bheetar rahi, jooti khat kapaal.*

*Rahiman dekh baren ko laghu na dijeye daar,*
*Jahan kaam aawe sooi, kaha kare talwaar.*

*Rahiman nij man ki bitha, man hi rakho goye,*
*Suni athley hain log sab, baanti na lehein koey.*

*Rahiman dhaga prem ka, mat toro chhitkaaey,*
*Toote se phir na mile, mile gaanth parti jaaey.*

*Rahiman nij sampati bina, kou na bipati sahay,*
*Binu paani jeon jalaj ko, nahin ravi sake bachaey.*

रहिमन तीर की चोट ते, चोट परे बचि जाय।
नैन बान की चोट ते, चोट परे मरि जाय।।

रहिमन छोटे नरन सों, होत बड़ो नहीं काम।
मढ़ो दमामो ना बने, सौ चूहे के चाम।।

रहिमन जिह्वा बावरी, कही गइ सरग पताल।
आपु तो कहि भीतर रही, जूती खत कपाल।।

रहिमन देख बड़ेन को, लघु न दीजिये डारि।
जहाँ काम आवे सुई, कहा करे तलवारि।।

रहिमन निज मन की बिथा, मन ही राखो गोय।
सुनि अठिलैहैं लोग सब, बाँटि न लैहैं कोय।।

रहिमन धागा प्रेम का, मत तोड़ो छिटकाय।
टूटे से फिर न मिले, मिले गाँठ परि जाय।।

रहिमन निज संपति बिना, कोउ न बिपति सहाय।
बिनु पानी ज्यों जलज को, नहिं रवि सकै बचाय।।

Water is a precious stuff, deserving to be stored,
None thrives without it — people, pearls or dough.

Bad company cannot but corrupt your mind,
Milk held in a drunkard's hand, passes for wine.

Our body is the winnowing fan to sift the world's grains,
Dicard thou the useless husk, the wholesome grain retain.

Welcome is the sable night which links us with our lord,
What use the sunny day which sunders us apart?

Vanquish pride and hunger, adopt humble ways,
Sweetness and humility, Rahiman, always win the day.

Money made by crooked ways vanishes in a wink,
As the flame of stolen wood, flares away and sinks.

Accursed are the folks, Rahim, who wield a begging bowl,
But worse are they who turn a beggar away from their door.

*Rahiman paani raakheye, bin paani sab soon,*
*Paani gaye na oobre, moti, maanush, choon.*

*Rahiman neechat sang basi, lagat kalank na kahi,*
*Doodh kalaari kar gahe, mad samujhe sab taahi.*

*Rahiman ya tan soop hai, leeje jagat pachhor,*
*Halukan ko uri jan de, garuey raakh bator.*

*Rahiman rajni hi bhali, piya se hoye milap,*
*Kharo divas kihi kaam ko, rahibo aapu aap.*

*Rahiman ris ko chhori ke karo ghareebi bhes,*
*Meetho bolo nai chalo, sabe tumharo des.*

*Rahiman vitt adharm ko jarat na laage baar,*
*Chori kari hori rachi, bhai tanik mein chhar.*

*Rahiman wey nar marchuke, je kahun maangat jaahin,*
*Un te pahle wahey mooey, jin mukh niksat naahin.*

रहिमन पानी राखिये, बिनु पानी सब सून।
पानी गए न ऊबरै, मोती, मानुष चून।।

रहिमन नीचत संग बसी, लगत कलंक न काहि।
दूध कलारी कर गहे, मद समुझै सब ताहि।।

रहिमन या तन सूप है, लीजै जगत पछोर।
हलुकन को उड़ि जान दै, गरुए राखि बटोर।।

रहिमन रजनी ही भली, पिय से होय मिलाप।
खरो दिवस किहि काम को, रहिबो आपुहि आप।।

रहिमन रिस को छौडि के, करौ गरीबी भेस।
मीठो बोलो नै चलो, सबै तुम्हारो देस।।

रहिमन वित्त अधर्म को, जरत न लागे बार।
चोरी करि होरी रची, भई तनिक में छार।।

रहिमन वे नर मर चुके, जे कहुँ माँगन जाहि।
उनते पहले वे मुए, जिन मुख निकसत नाहि।।

Everyone whom we meet greets us as a matter of course,
Only when we need some help, we can know a friend from foe.

Everyman gives respect to a man of state and wealth,
None but God helps a man, sans a friend, starved of pelf.

There's a time to ripen, a time to fade and fall,
Nothing stays the same, Rahim, why regret at all.

He who doesn't provide a shade, nor yields a fruit,
Upwards like a palm he shoots, without being of use.

Make love your guiding star, it will lend a glow to life,
When turmeric blends with dough, one sheds its pale, the other its white.

Keep away from marriage, Rahim, 'it's a dread disease,
With the beat of drums and timbrels, you are bound hand and feet.

Difficult is the path of love, beyond the might of common clay,
It is to ride a restive horse, and push it into the burning bay.

*Sab ko sab kou hare, kei salaam, kei Ram,*
*Hit Rahim tab jaaneye jab kuchh atke kaam.*

*Samay dasa kul dekh ke, sabekarat sanmaan,*
*Rahiman deen anaath ko, tum bin ko bhagwan.*

*Samay paaey phal hot hai, samay paaey jhar jaaey,*
*Sada rahe nahin ek hi, ka Rahim pachhtaaey.*

*Hoey na jaki chhain dhig, phal Rahim ati door,*
*Barhun so bin kaaj hi, jaise taar khajoor.*

*Rahiman preet saraheye, mile hot rang doon,*
*Jeon hardi jardi taje, taje safedi choon.*

*Rahiman beaah bayaadh hai, sako tau chaaho bachaey,*
*Paan mein beri parat hai, dhol bajaey bajaey.*

*Rahiman maen turang charh, chalwo padak maanhi,*
*Prem panth aiso kathin, sab so nibhat naanhi.*

सबको सब कोऊ करे, कै सलाम, कै राम।
हित रहीम तब जानिए, जब कछु अटके काम।।

समय दसा कुल देखि कै, सबै करत सनमान।
रहिमन दीन अनाथ को, तुम बिन को भगवान।।

समय पाय फल होत है, समय पाय झरि जाय।
सदा रहे नहिं एक सी, का रहीम पछिताय।।

होय न जाकी छाँह ढिग, फल रहीम अति दूर।
बढ़िहू सो बिनु काज ही, जैसे तार खजूर।।

रहिमन प्रीति सराहिये, मिले होत रंग दून।
ज्यों हरदी जरदी तजे, तजे सफेदी चून।।

रहिमन व्याह बियाधि है, सकौ तो चाहु बचाय।
पांय में बेड़ी परत है, ढ़ोल बजाय बजाय।।

रहिमन मैन तुरंग चढ़ि, चीलवो पादक माहिं।
प्रेमपंथ एसो कठिन, सबसों निबहत नाहिं।।

It is He who giveth us unasked, unsought,
We feel embarrassed when thanked for naught.

Love doesn't accept the rule of simple give and take,
Unconcerned with consequence, it puts its life at stake.

The great do not fall in stature if you call them small,
"Girdhar" called the "flute-player", still remains the Lord.

There was a time when we disliked even a garland that divides,
Ah, the change, now we lie sundered by the mounains high.

Even the rich, hunger-pressed, beg from door to door,
As people take to digging wells, when the river dries at source.

Many a time I tell my belly: "Better be my back,"
"When empty, you make me beg, when stuffed, you make me brag."

Fear of teacher, tribe, or family, fear of losing fame,
He whom these fears possess,worships in the spiritual fane.

*Den haar koi aur hai, bhajat hain din ren,*
*Log bharam hum par dharen, ya te neeche nain.*

*Yeh na Rahim saraaheye len den ki pareet,*
*Pranan baaji raakheye, haar hoey ke jeet.*

*Jo baren ko laghu kahen, nahin Rahim dhar jaahein,*
*Girdhar murlidhar kahe, kachhu dukh maanat naahin.*

*Rahiman ek din wah rahe, beech na sohat haar,*
*Vayoo ju aisi bah gai, beechan tare pahaar.*

*Rahiman daani daridre tar, tau jaanchbe yog,*
*Jeon saritan sookha pare, kuaan khudawan log.*

*Rahiman kaht supet son, kyon na bhayo tu peeth,*
*Bhooke bheek mangawai, bhare digaawe deeth.*

*Ghar dar, guru dar, bans dar, dar lajja, dar maan,*
*Dar jehi ke ji mein base, tin paya rahmaan.*

देनदार कोई और है, भेजत है दिन रैन।
लोग भरम हम पर धरै, यातें नीचे नैन।।

यह न रहीम सराहिये, लेन-देन की प्रीत।
प्रानन बाजी राखिये, हार होय कै जीत।।

जो बड़ेन को लघु कहें, नहीं रहीम घटि जाहिं।
गिरिधर मुरलीधर कहे, कछु दुख मानत नाहिं।।

रहिमन एक दिन वे रहे, बीच न सोहत हार।
बायु जुं ऐसी बह गई, बीजन तरे पहाड़।।

रहिमन दानि दरिद्र तर, तऊ जांचवे योग।
ज्यों सरितन सूखा परे, कुंआं खुदावत लोग।।

रहिमन कहत सुपेट सों, क्यों न भयो तू पीठ।
भूखे भीक मंगावइ, भरे डिगावे डीठि।।

घर-डर, गुरु डर, बंस डर, डर लज्जा, डर मान।
डर जेही के जी में बसे, तिन पाया रहमान।।

When he flung his load in fire, Rahim was able to cross the bar,
Those burdened with their baggage, were left in mid-stream, tempest-tossed

To express your need to others is a task lacking grace,
The bride of a noble home is shy to visit a stranger's place.

Where love, regard and respect abound, that is the place to stay,
Where these things diminish, quit that place without delay.

Till I have my limbs intact, why to beg or beseech,
The reflcction cast in the river, doesn't wet our hands and feet.

You will get something from him, from whom you have some hope,
How can a river, sand-dry, slake our thirsty throat?

These four heed not the pleas and prayers you make:
Creditor, king, beggar, and a sensual maid.

Rahim is now a vagrant, begging from door to door,
Renounce, friends, his company, he is Rahim no more.

*Bhaarjhonk ke bhaar mein, Rahim utre paar,*
*Pe doobe manjhdaar mein,jinke sir par bhaar.*

*Garj aapni aap son , Rahiman kahi na jaaey,*
*Jaise kul ki kulbadhu, par ghar jaat lajaaey.*

*Rahiman tab lag tharieye, daan, maan, sanmaan,*
*Ghatat maan dekheye jabhin, turathi kareye payaan.*

*Jo Rahim tan haath hai, mansa kahun kinj aahin,*
*Jal mein jo chhaa paro,kaaya bheejat naahin.*

*Tason hi kuchh paaeye, keeje ja ki aas,*
*Rete sarwar par gaey, kaise bujhe payaas?*

*Arj garj maane nahin, Rahiman eh jan chaar,*
*Rinia, raja, maangta, kaam aaturi naar.*

*Yeh Rahim dar dar phire, maang madhu kari khaan,*
*Yaaro yaari chhaad deo, wah Rahim ab naahn.*

भार झोंक के भाड़ में, रहीम उतरै पार।
पे डूबे मंझधार में, जिनके सिर भार।।

गर्ज आपनी आप सों, रहिमन कही न जाय।
जैसे कुल की कुलवधू, पर घर जात लजाय।।

रहिमन तब तक ठहरिए, दान मान सनमान।
घटत मान देखिए जबी, तुरत करिए पयान।।

जो रहीम तन हाथ है, मनसा कहूं किन जाहिं।
जल में जो छांह पड़ो, काया भीजत नाहि।।

तासों ही कुछ पाइये, कीजै या की आस।
रेते सखर पर गये, कैसे गुझे प्यास।।

अरज गरज मानै नहीं, रहिमन ये जन चार।
रिनिया, राजा, मंगता, काम अतूरी नार।।

यह रहीम दर दर फिरै, मांग मधुकरी खान।
यारो यारी छड़ दियो, वह रहीम अब ना।।

# Varind Kavi
**(1700–1780)**

# Varind Kavi (1700–1780)

Authentic details about Varind Kavi's life are not easily available. He was, it is generally agreed, born in or about 1700. His full name was Varindavan Das. His father Roopji was a poet in his own right and a deeply religious man, a devotee of Hindu gods and goddesses, including goddess Saraswati who is said to have granted the boon of poetry-writing to Roopji and his descendents. Roopji had first lived at Bikaner, and later shifted to Merhta, which was also the birthplace of Varind. Varind had thus inherited his poetic talent from his father, and developed it through self-effort and God's grace. At the age of ten he was sent to Kashi for education, where he sat at the feet of the famous Sanskrit teacher and scholar, Pt Tara ji, who gave him lessons in Sanskrit and Vedanta, and initiated him into the art of poetry writing. Varind broadened the field of his knowledge and experience through extensive travels to different places in the country. Among the places he visited may be mentioned Jodhpur and Kashi, Delhi, Pushkar and Dbaka in Bengal, Anandpur Sahib and Lahore in the Punjab. He visited Anandpur Sahib at a time when Guru Gobind Singh was engaged in the task of consolidating the Khalsa Panth.He had also enjoyed for a shortwhile the status of the court poet in the court of Guru Gobind Singh. We can trace eulogistic references to Gobind Singh in his poetry of those days. Surprising as it may seem, he was also connected with the court of Aurangzeb, and his son Azim-ul-Shaan, who, in religion and politics, stood on the opposite pole of Guru Gobind Singh. Yet he was not a sychophant, but a self-respecting man. When Aurangzeb, fired by his fanatic zeal had started breaking the Hindu temples, Varind had boldly criticised him through his verse. Towards the end of his life, Varind had moved to Kishengarh, where he enjoyed the patronage of Raja Raj Singh and lived till the time of his death in 1780.

A man of learning and ability, Varind was sought after by rajas and aristocrats as a private tutor, and was highly respected for his poetic ability. His connection with Aurangzeb and his son had spread his reputation in the aristocratic circles. He was also the tutor of raja Rajsingh of Kishengarh who, like other aristocrats, had given him land in appreciation of his services as a poet and teacher. It was at Kishengarh that he had translated the Hitupdesh and written a collection of *dohas* called: *Akhsharadi Dohas*. He died at Kishengarh in 1780.

Varind had an impressive personality. Dressed in a Rajasthani *angrakha*, and a turban on his head, a *mojri* covering his feet, a sword hanging round his shoulders, a long moustache spread over his upper lip, Varind looked a self-confident man of power and position, a courtier and a poet who would not flinch from a fight to defend his honour and pride.

Varind was the author of the following compositions:

(*i*) Sammet Shiksha Chhand,

(*ii*) Barah Maasa,

(*iii*) Aksharadi Dohe,

(*iv*) Nain Bateesi,

(*v*) Bhaar Panchashika,

(*vi*) Shringar Shiksha,

(*vii*) Pawan Pacheesi,

(viii) Hitopadeshak,

(*ix*) Pushkarahtak,

(x) Bhasha Hitopdesh,

(*xi*) Neet Satsai,

(*xii*) Bachanika or Roop Singh ki Vaarta,

(*xiii*) Yaqmak Satsai,

(*xiv*) Sat Swaroop

# DOHAS OF VARIND KAVI

Pleasant words sound unpleasant, if spoken out of place,
Sounds of love in times of war unwelcome music make.

Common jokes, timely told, a good response evoke,
As abuse, at wedding feasts, passes for a joke.

A lover sees no fault in his darling mate,
The cowherd friends of sable Shyam call him rosy-faced.

Approach only those for help who have the means to help,
How can a pond, stark dry, pacify your thirst?

Fruitless is our strife and stir, if not blessed by God,
A smiling field, rich and ripe, can still to locusts fall.

Weigh your worth, assess your skill, ere you undertake a task,
It's a saying, wise and old: cut your coat to match your cloth.

How can the poor serfs afford to offend their mighty lords,
Can the water-dwelling fish, engage the crocodiles in war?

*Neeki pe pheeki lage, bin awsar ki baat,*
*Jaise barnat yudh mein, nahin singaar suhaat.*

*Pheeki pe neeki lage, kahieye samay vichaar,*
*Sabko man harshit kare, jeon vivah mein gaar.*

*Raagi awgun na gine, yehi jagat ki chaal,*
*Dekho, sab hi Shyam ko, kahat gawalan lal.*

*Jaahi te kuchh paaeye, karieye ta ki aas,*
*Reete sarwar par gaye, kaise bujhe payaas!*

*Kaha hoey udham kieye,jo Prabhu hi pratikool,*
*Jaise upje khet ko, kara salbh nirmool.*

*Apni pahunch vichari ke, kartab karieye daur,*
*Tete paanv pasaareye, jeti laambi saur.*

*Kaise nibhen nibal jan, kar sablan son ghair,*
*Jaise bas saagar vishay, kara magar son ber.*

नीकी पै फीकी लगे, बिन अवसर की बात।
जैसे बरनत युद्ध में, नहिं सिंगार सुहात।।

फीकी पे नीकी लगे, कहिए समय विचारि।
सब को मन हर्षित करै, ज्यों विवाह में गारि।।

रागी अवगुन ना गिनै, यही जगत की चाल।
देखे, सबही श्याम को, कहत ग्वालन लाल।।

जाही ते कछु पाइये, करिये ताकी आस।
रीते सरवर पर गये, कैसे बुझत पिआस।।

कहा होय उद्दम किये, जो प्रभु ही प्रतिकूल।
जैसे उपजे खेत को, करत सलभ निरमूल।।

अपनी पहुँच बिचारिकै, करतब करिये दौर।
तेते पाँव पसारिये, जेती लाँबी सौर।।

कैसे निबहै निबल जन, करि सबलन सो गैर।
जैसे बस सागर बिषै, करत मगर सों बैर।।

Who can gather wealth and knowledge without striving hard?
The fan giveth no breeze, unless you whirl it fast.

If an issue is getting resolved, do not let it get involved,
Adjust your sails to suit the wind, change the course of your bark.

Always seek the company wise, of people good and great,
Depending upon the tree it climbs, the creeper takes its shape.

Frank advice sounds bitter, you should heed it still,
Serious illness, for its cure, needs a bitter pill.

Who can help or heal a man trapped by fate hostile,
The lotus hiding from the blaze, dies of cold inside.

Business based on fraud or cunning, cannot long survive,
You cannot put a wooden vessel on the fire twice.

Truly do the eyes reflect the happenings of the heart,
As a mirror reflects your face, showing all its warts.

*Vidya, dhan udham bina kaho jo paawe kaun,*
*Bina dulaey na mile jeon pankhe ki paun.*

*Banti dekh banaieye, parn na deeje khot,*
*Jaise chale bayaar tab, tesi deeje oat.*

*Rahe sameep baren ke, hot baro hit-male,*
*Sabhi jaanat barhat hai, braksh barabar bel.*

*Bure lagat sikh ke bachan, hieye vicharo aap,*
*Karwi bheshaj bin pieye, mite na tan ki taap.*

*Bidhi roothe tuthe kaban, ko kar sake sahaey,*
*Ban-gat-bhayjalgat nalin, tahn hit det jaraey.*

*Pher nahain hai kapat son, jo kijeye beopaar,*
*Jaise haandi kaath ki, charhe na dooji baar.*

*Naina det bataey sab, hit ko het ahet,*
*Jaise nirmal aarsi, bhali buri kahi det.*

विद्या धन उद्यम बिना, कहो जो पावै कौन।
बिना डुलाये ना मिलै, ज्यों पंखा की पौन।।

बनती देख्र बनाइये, परन न दीजै खोट।
जैसी चलै बयार तब, तैसी दीजै ओट।।

रहे समीप बड़ेन के, होत बड़ो हित-मेल।
सबही जानत बढ़त है, बृच्छ बराबर बेल।।

बुरे लगत सिख्र के बचन, हिये विचारो आप।
करूई भेषज बिन पिये, मिटै न तन की ताप।।

विधि रूठे तूठे कवन, को करि सके सहाय।
बन-गत-भय जलगत नलिन, तहं हित देत जराय।।

फेर नाहीं है कपट सों, जो कीजै व्यापार।
जैसे हांडी काठ की, चढ़ै न दूजी बार।।

नैना देत बताय सब, हित को हेत अहेत।
जैसे निर्मल आरसी, भली बुरी कहि देत।।

What good is that pleasure which entails grief,
Better burn away the gold that makes your ears bleed.

None is either good or bad, when mute and mum are one and all,
You can know a crow from lark, when spring arrives in grove and park.

Do not lionize a man ere you weigh his worth,
Hordes of wolves in lamb's clothing stalk upon this earth.

Let not his colour or shape a man's worth decide,
The cow's milk and cactus-juice are not the same, though white.

Do not on a stupid man words of wisdom waste,
The noseless man, shown a mirror, tends to fly in rage.

Be ye not obdurate, it only gives offence,
Heavier grows the blanket as it gets drenched.

Sweet words can quieten down tempers hot and rude,
As a drop of water cool, boiling milk subdues.

*Kareye sukh ko hot dukh, yeh kahu kaun sayaan,*
*Wa sone ko jaareye, jaason toote kaan.*

*Bhale bure sab ek se, jaulon bolat naahin,*
*Jaan parat hain kaak pik, ritu basant ke maanhi.*

*Na kari naam rang dekhi sam, gun bin samjhe baat,*
*Gaat ghat gau-doodh te, sehur ke te ghaat.*

*Hithu ko kaheye na tihi, jo nar hoey abodh,*
*Jeon nakte ko aarsi, hot dikhaey karodh.*

*Bin gun kul jaae bina, maan na kari manuhaar,*
*Thagat phirat sab jagat ko, bhesh bhagat ko dhaar.*

*Ati hath mat kar hath barhe, baat na kari hai koey,*
*Jeon jeon bheeje kaamri, teon, teon bhaari hoey.*

*Madhu bachan te jaat mit, uttam jan abhimaan,*
*Tanik seet jal son mite, jaise doodh-ufaan.*

करिये सुख्र को होत दुख्र, यह कहु कौन सयान।
वा सोने को जारिये, जासों टूटे कान।।

भले बुरे सब एक से, जौंलो बोलत नाहिं।
जान परत हैं काक पिक, ऋतु बसन्त के माहिं।।

न करि नाम रंग देखि सम, गुन बिन समझे बात।
गात धात गो दूध ते, सेहुड़ के ते घात।।

हितहू को कहिये न तिहि, जो नर होय अबोध।
ज्यों नकटे को आरसी, होत दिख्राये क्रोध।।

बिन गुन कुल जाने बिना, मान न करि मनुहारि।
ठगत फिरत सब जगत को, भेष भक्त को धारि।।

अति हठ मत कर हठ बढ़े, बात न करि है कोय।
ज्यों-ज्यों भीजै कामरी, त्यों-त्यों भारी होय।।

मधुर बचन ते जात मिट, उत्तम जन अभिमान।
तनिक सीत जल सो मिटै, जैसे दूध-उफान।।

When we cannot fight the strong, we terrorize the weak,
The gale makes no dent on rocks, but bows down the trees.

Everyone supports the rich, the poor beseech in vain,
The wind fans the bigger fire, kills the candle flame.

The wicked will be wicked still, howsoever good you be,
Collyrium cannot turn white, how hard you may bleach.

If all covet the same thing, it leads to fatal feuds,
Princes commit fratricide to monopolize their rule

He who cares for others' pleasure, also shares their pain,
Water cools down the fire, wind ignites again.

A beauteous face and virtuous soul is something hard to meet,
You can't have a bar of gold, with sweet scent replete.

We are none to interfere, God's will prevails,
The Master manipulates the lyre, as he likes, plays.

*Kuchh basaey nahin sabal son, kare nirbal par zor,*
*Chale na achal ukhari taru, darat pawan jhakor.*

*Sabe sahayk sabal ke, kou na nirbal sahaey,*
*Pawan jagawat aag ko, deephi det bujhaey.*

*Dusht na chhore dusht-ta, kaisehun sukh det,*
*Dhoyehun sau ber ke, kaajar hoey na set.*

*Abhilashi ik baat ke, tin mein hoey virodh,*
*Kaaj raaj ke raajsut, larat bhirat kar karodh.*

*Jo jako chahe bhalo, so taahi ki pir,*
*Neer bujhawat aag ko, sokhe tahi sameer.*

*Jaise gun deeno dai, taiso roop nibandh,*
*Yeh dono kahn paaeye, sono aur sugand.*

*Jo chaho soi karo, mero kuchh na kahav,*
*Jantari ke kar jantar hain, bhaawe soi bajav.*

कछु बसाय नहि सबल सों, करै निबल पर जोर।
चलै न अचल उखारि तरु, डारत पवन झकोर।।

सबै सहायक सबल के, कोउ न निबल सहाय।
पवन जगावत आग को, दीपहिं देत बुझाय।।

दुष्ट न छांडे दुष्टता, कैसेहूं सुख देत।
धोयेहूं सौ बेर के, काजर होय न सेत।।

अभिलाषी इक बात के, तिनमें होय विरोध।
काज राज को राजसुत, लरत भिरत करि क्रोध।।

जो जाको चाहै भलो, सो ताही की पीर।
नीर बुझावत आग को, सोखे ताहि समीर।।

जैसे गुन दीनों दई, तैसो रुप निबन्ध।
ये दोनों कहं पाइये, सोनों और सुगन्ध।।

जो चाहो सोई करो, मेरो कछु न कहाव।
जन्त्री के कर जन्त्र हैं, भावै सोइ बजाव।।

Improve your worth, enrich your soul, forget about the surface show,
You cannot sell a dry cow, even if you trumpets blow.

Nothing can change our nature, inbuilt, ingrained,
Bitter gall, honey-steeped, retains its venom all he same.

Pain departing, brings in pleasure, pleasure gone, pain arrives,
As night receding brings the day, the day departing, night.

Love and joy cannot be hid, the face reflects them both,
As a scent-stealing man, is by his smell exposed.

Strongest are the bonds of love, unique, non-pareil
The bumble-bee which cuts through trees, falls for the lotus frail.

Whichever thing promotes our good, wins our love and praise,
A love-lorn maiden loves the crow which all the world doth hate.

Self-interest is the force that motivates our lives,
The birds love a juicy plant, reject a tree sterile.

*Aadumber taji kijeye, gun-sangrah chit chaey,*
*Chhir rahit gau na bike, aaniya ghant bandhaey.*

*Nahin ilaaj dekheo suneo, jason mitat subhav,*
*Madhu-pat kotik det tau, vish na tajat vish bhav.*

*Sukh beete dukh hot hai, dukh beete sukh hot,*
*Divas gaey jeon nisi udit, nisigat divas-udot.*

*Nabal, anand, umang, dure na mukh chakh aur,*
*Taiso jaaneo jaat hai, jeon sugandh ka chor.*

*Jaise bandhan prem ko, taiso bandh na aur,*
*Kathin bhede kamal ko, chhed na nikre bhaur.*

*Kou kahe hit ki kahe, hon taahi son het,*
*Sabhe urawat kaag ko, pe birhan bal det.*

*Swarath ke sab hi sage, bin swarath kou naahin,*
*Sabe panchhi saras taru, niras bhaye uri jaahin.*

आडम्बर तजि कीजिए, गुण-संग्रह चित चाय।
छीर रहित गउ ना बिकै, आनिय घंट बंधाय।।

नहिं इलाज देख्यो, सुन्यौ, जासो मिटत सुभाव।
मधु-पट कोटिक देत तऊ, विष न तजत विष भाव।।

सुख बीते दुःख होत है, दुःख बीते सुख होत।
दिवस गये ज्यौं निसि उदित, निसिगत दिवस-उदोत।।

नवल आनंद-उमंग, दुरै न मुख चख ओर।
तैसो जान्यो जात है, ज्यों सुगन्ध की छोर।।

जैसे बन्धन प्रेम को, तैसो बन्ध न और।
काठहिं भेदै कमल को, छेद न निकर्र भौंर।।

कोउ कहे हित की कहे, हों ताहि सों हेत।
सबै उड़ावत काग को, पे बिरहन बलि देत।।

स्वारथ के सब ही सगे, बिन स्वारथ कोउ नाहिं।
सेवै पंछी सरस तरु, निरस भये उड़ि जाहिं।।

Be not be blunt in your speech, it may cause offence,
A blind man, when called blind, cannot but resent.

God assigns a specific role to everything He makes,
Tongue cannot hear the sound, ears cannot prate.

No amount of imitation can make a man great,
How can a crow ever acquire the swan's gentle grace.

Keep away from vicious folk, their company can deprave,
Milk poured by the wine-seller, acquires the smell of ale.

Even gods show no mercy to the weaker folks,
People sacrifice the lamb, dread the lion that roars.

Company of the noble souls brings joy untold,
When a king perfumes his robes, fragrance fills the court.

People put up with the fool in the absence of the wise,
Who would care for the taper when the sun arrives!

*Dosh bhari na uchaareye jadpi jatharath baat,*
*Kahe andh ko aandhro, maan buro satraal.*

*Brahm banaey ban rahe, te phir aur bane na,*
*Kaan kaht nahin ben jeon, jeebh sunat nahin ben.*

*Uttam jan ki hor kar, neech na hot rasaal,*
*Kauwa kaise chal sake, rajhans ki chaal.*

*Jehin parsang dooshan lage, tajieyo tako saath,*
*Madira maanat hai jagat, doodh kalari haath.*

*Harat devhu nibal aru, durbal hi ke pran,*
*Baagh sinh ko chhodke, det chhag balidaan.*

*Uttam jan ke sang mein, sahje hi sukh-bhaas,*
*Jaise narip laawe atar, let sabha-jan baas.*

*Moorh tahan hi maaneye, jahan na pandit hoey,*
*Deepak ko ravi ke uday, baat na poochhe koey.*

दोष-भरी न उचारिये, जदपि जथारथ बात।
कहे अन्ध को आंधरो, मान बुरो सतराल।।

ब्रह्म बनाये बन रहे, ते फिर और बनैं न।
कान कहत नहिं बैन ज्यों, जीभ सुनत नहिं बैन।।

उत्तम जन की होड़ करि, नीच न होत रसाल।
कौवा कैसे चल सके, राजहंस की चाल।।

जिहिं प्रसंग दूषन लगे, तजियो ताको साथ।
मदिरा मानत है जगत, दूध कलारी हाथ।।

हरत दैवहू निबल अरू, दुर्बल ही के प्रान।
बाघ सिंह को छांडिके, देत छाग बलिदान।।

उत्तम जन के संग में, सहजै ही सुख-भास।
जैसे नृप लावे अतर, लेत सभा जन बास।।

मूढ़ तहां ही मानिये, जहां न पण्डित होय।
दीपक को रवि के उदै, बात न पूछे कोय।।

If it serves our selfish end, we do not mind the painful pricks,
A milch cow is fed and pampered, even if it stamps and kicks.

A virtue doesn't lose its worth, if fools refuse to recognise,
How can you blame the sunny day, if owls can't perceive the light.

Evil must on you recoil, no escape at all,
He who digs a pit for others, himself therein falls.

Our personal goal determines, what we like, dislike,
A thief loves the dark, dreads the moonlit night.

Put your wealth to proper use, for personal need, or public use,
Do not, like a stagnant pool, let it rot or stink unsed.

Be not simple and straight, let the forests make you wise,
Tall trees are chopped down, slanting ones survive.

Pain and suffering make no dent on the noble minds,
The more you heat and melt the gold, the more it gets refined.

*Bin swarath kaise sahey kou karuwe bain,*
*Laat khaat puchkaareye, hoey dulharu dhen.*

*Moorakh gun samujhen nahin, to an guni mein chook,*
*Kaha bhayo din ko bibhau, dekhe jo na aluk.*

*Hoey burai ten buro, yeh keeno nirdhaar,*
*Khaar khanego aur ko, ta ko koop tayyaar.*

*Ja ko janh swarath sadhe, soi tahi suhat,*
*Chor na payari chandni, jaise kaari raat.*

*Dhan sancheo kahi kaam ka, khau kharch hari pareet,*
*Bandhyo gandhilo koop jal, karhe barhe yeh reet.*

*Ati hi sarl na hojeo, dekho jeon banrai,*
*Seedhe seedhe chhedieye, baanko taru bach jaaey.*

*Kasht prehun sadhujan, neku na hot malaan,*
*Jeon jeon kanchan taaeye, teon teon nirmal jaan.*

बिन स्वारथ कैसे सहै, कोउ करुवे बैन।
लात खाय पुचकारिये, होय दुधारु धैन।।

मूरख गुन समुझें नहीं, तो न गुनी में चूक।
कहा भयो दिन को बिभौं, देखै जो न उलूक।।

होय बुराई तें बुरो, यह कीनो निरधार।
खाड़ खनैगो और को, ताको कूप तैयार।।

जाको जहं स्वारथ सधै, सोई ताहि सुहात।
चोर न प्यारी चांदनी, जैसे कारी रात।।

धन संच्यो किहि काम को, खाउ स्वरच हरि प्रीति।
बंध्यौ गंधीलो कूप जल, कढ़ै बढ़ै यहि रीति।।

अति ही सरल न हूजियो, देखो ज्यों बनराय।
सीधे-सीधे छेदिये, बांको तरु बच जाय।।

कष्ठ परेहूं साधुजन, नैकु न होत मलान।
ज्यों-ज्यों कंचन ताइये, त्यों-त्यों निर्मल जान।।

Grain by grain you make a maund, spend it, lo, it flies,
Drop by drop the pot doth fill, a little leak can drain it dry.

The wicked loves his wickedness, the sinner sin adores,
The leech sucks the blood of cow, but vital milk abhors.

Things take time to ripen, haste serves no end,
The plant fructifies on time, howsoever hard you tend.

A coward remains a coward still, let him don the hero's robes,
A jackal flaunting lion-skin, soon gets exposed.

It's easy to spend the wealth by others' sweat stored,
A partridge gulps down at once, what ants slowly hoard.

Relax not your own attempt, when you see the succour arrive,
Break not the water pitcher,if the clouds fill the sky.

We should neither befriend the mean, nor antagonize,
Pernicious are his kisses, fatal is his bite.

*Kan kan jore man jure, kaarhe nibre soey,*
*Boond-boond jeon ghat bhare, tapkat beete toey.*

*Doshhin ko umhe gahe, gun na gahe khal lok,*
*Pieye rudhir, pe na pieye.lagi pyodhar jonk.*

*Karaj dheere hot hai, kaahe hot adheer,*
*Samay paaey taruwar phare, ketak seencho neer.*

*Bhesh banaey sur ko, kaayar sur na soey,*
*Khaal urhaaey sinh ki, sayyaar sinh nahin hoey.*

*Saanchi sampati aur ki, aur bhogven aaey,*
*Kan-sangrah chetin ko, jeon teetar chugi jaaey.*

*Udham kabhun na chhdieye, par aasa ke mod,*
*Gagar kaise phoreye, uneo dekh payod.*

*Hithu bhalo na neech ko, naahin bhalo ahet,*
*Chaat apawan tan kare, kaat swan dukh det.*

कन-कन जोरै मन जुरै, काढै निबरै सोय।
बूंद-बूंद ज्यों घट भरै, टपकत बीतै तोय।।

दोषहिं को उमहै गहै, गुन न गहै खल-लोक।
पियै रुधिर, पय न पियै, लगी पयोधर जोंक।।

कारज धीरे होत है, काहे होत अधीर।
समय पाय तरुवर फरै, केतिक सींचौ नीर।।

भेष बनाये सूर कौ, कायर सूर न सोय।
खाल उढ़ाये सिंह की, स्यार सिंह नहिं होय।।

सांची संपति और की, और भोगवैं आय।
कन-संग्रह चैंटीन को, ज्यों तीतर चुगि जाय।।

उद्यम कबहुं न छांड़िये, पर आसा के मोद।
गागर कैसे फोरिये, उनयो देखि पयोद।।

हितू भलो न नीच को, नाहिंन भले अहेत।
चाट अपावन तन करे, काट स्वान दुख देत।।

Noble souls live for others, selfishness eschew,
Annapoorna feeds the world, her lord begs for food.

A fool doesn't fit into the company of the wise,
A crane in the flock of swans, presents a queer sight.

You can try and test a man in time of need alone,
Gold has to pass through fire ere its worth be known.

Company of the good delights, the vicious folks offend,
Go, visit a perfumer's shop, then a blacksmith's den.

Everyone in this world has his limits prescribed,
A lamp cannot, like the sun, flood the world with light.

They are fools who believe they alone can run this show,
As if the sun cannot rise, unless the cock crows.

Assess your strength, weigh your worth, ere you undertake a task,
A dwarf need not stretch his arms, to pluck the fruit hung aloft.

*Uttam par karaj kare,apno kaam bisaar,*
*Poore annjahan ko, ta pati bhikshadhaar.*

*Chatur sabha mein koor nar, sobha pawat naahin,*
*Jaise bak sohat nahin, hans mandali maanhin.*

*Kaam parei jaaneye, jo nar jaiso hoey,*
*Bin taaey khoto kharo, gahno lakhe na koey.*

*Hot susangati sahj sukh, dukh kusang ke than,*
*Gandhi aur lohar ki, dekho baith dukaan.*

*Hoey pahunch jake jitni, teto karat parkash,*
*Ravi jeon kaise kari sake, deepak tam ko naas.*

*Hoey na karaj mo bina, yeh jo kahe so ayaan,*
*Jahan na kukkar shabd tehn, hot na tahaan bihan.*

*Peechhe karaj kijeye, pahile pahunch pasaar,*
*Kaise aawat uch phal, bawan baanh pasaar!*

उत्तम पर कारज करै, अपनो काम बिसार।
पूरे अन्न जहान कौ, ता पति भिक्षाधार।।

चतुर सभा में कूर नर, सोभा पावत नाहिं।
जैसे बक सोहत नहीं, हंस मंडली मांहि।।

काम परेई जानिए, जो नर जैसो होय।
बिन ताये खोटो खरो, गहनो लखे न कोय।।

होत सुसंगति सहज सुख, दुख कुसंग के थान।
गन्धी और लुहार की, देखौ बैठि दुकान।।

होय पहुंच जाकी जिती, तेतौ करत प्रकास।
रवि ज्यों कैसे करि सकै, दीपक तम को नास।।

होय न कारज मो बिना, यह जु कहै सु अयान।
जहां न कुक्कुट सब्द तहं, होत न तहां बिहान।।

पीछे कारज कीजिए, पहिले पहुंच पसार।
कैसे आवत उच्च फल, बावन बांह पसार।।

Do not under-rate your foe, you may come to harm,
A little spark, if ignored, can burn away the barn.

People try every source to realize their goal,
But none cares for medicine, when health gets restored.

Company of the noble souls melts away your dross,
As brackish sea with clouds conjoined, produces sweet drops.

Everyone rules the roost in his time and place,
On river, the boat supports the bus, on road, reverse prevails.

A mean man is dangerous, both in love and rage,
Water, be it cold or hot, puts down the blaze.

Yogis think of naught else when they meditate,
As an acrobat on rope, on rope alone concentrates.

*Ari chhoto janeye nahin, jaate hoey bigaar,*
*Teen-samooh ko chhinak mein, jaarat tanik angaar.*

*Nar karaj ki siddhi lau, kare anek parkaar,*
*Chhoote rog sareer ten, ko dhoonde upchaar.*

*Uttam jan son milat hi, awgun hun gun hoey,*
*Ghan sang kharo uda dhi mili, barse meetho toey.*

*Apni apni thaur par sabko laage daaw,*
*Jal mein gari naav par, thal gari par naav.*

*Ka ras ka rios mein, ari son jaani patiaey,*
*Jaise seetal tapatjal, daarat aag bujhaey.*

*Bhajat nirantar sant-jan, haripad chit lagaey,*
*Jaise nat darirh dara shti kari, dharat barat par paaey.*

अरि छोटो जानिये नहीं, जाते होय बिगार।
तृन-समूह को छिनक में, जारत तनिक अंगार।।

नर कारज की सिद्धि लौ, करै अनेक प्रकार।
छूटे रोग सरीर तैं, को ढूंढै उपचार।।

उत्तम जन सों मिलत ही, अवगुन हूं गुन होय।
धन संग खारो उदधि मिलि, बरसै मीठो तोय।।

अपनी-अपनी ठौर पर, सबको लागे दाव।
जल में गाड़ी नाव पर, थल गाड़ी पर नाव।।

का रस का रोस में, अरि सों जनि पतियाय।
जैसे सीतल तप्त जल, डारत आगि बुझाय।।

भजत निरन्तर सन्त जन, हरि-पद चित्त लगाय।
जैसे नट दृढ़, दृष्टि करि, धरत बरत पर पाय।।

How can he give in charity who doesn't own a thing,
The naked bathing on the pool, has nothing to wash or wring.

People tell blatant lies to boost their image,
A pros cuts down her years, a saint extends his age.

That which subserves your need, let that source stay,
Never cut down the branch on which you swing and sway.

Even the smaller minds improve mixing with the good and great,
The Ganga sanctifies the sludge, that mixes with its waves.

Men of honour undertake no demeaning task,
Even if it dies of hunger, the lion never eats the grass.

Leave a poor man alone, provoke not his rage,
If you kick the way-side dust, it will rise up in your face.

Love and worth when combined, bring renown and fame,
As wick and oil put together, help to light the flame.

*Jo dhanwant su dey kuchh, dey kahan dhanheen,*
*Kahan nichore nagan jan, nahan sarovar keen.*

*Apni parabhuta ko sabhe, bolat jhoot banaey,*
*Baisya bas ghatavahi, jogi baras barhaey.*

*Tahi ko kareye jatan, rahieye jinhı adhaar,*
*Ko kaate ta daar ko, baithe jahi daar.*

*Neechhu uttam sang mili, uttam hi huve jaaey,*
*Gag-sang jal nidhu, gangodak ke bhaey.*

*Kare na kabhun sahsi, deen heen ko kaaj,*
*Bhook sahe pe ghaas ko, nahin bhakhe marigraj.*

*Heenjaan na virodheye, wa tau tan dukhdaey,*
*Rajhu thokar maareye, charhe sees par aaey.*

*Gun sneh-jut hot hain, tahi ki chhabi hot,*
*Gun sneh ke deep ki, jaise jyoti udot.*

जो धनवन्त सु देय कछु, देय कंहा धनहीन।
कंहा निचोरै नगन जन, न्हान सरोवर कीन।।

अपनी प्रभुता को सबै, बोलत झूठ बनाय।
बेस्या बरस घटावही, जोगी बरस बढ़ाय।।

ताही को करिये जतन, रहिये जिहिं आधार।
को काटै ता डार को, बैठे जाही डार।।

नीचहु उत्तम संग मिलि, उत्तम ही ह्वै जाय।
गग-संग जल निंद्यहू, गंगोदक के भाय।।

करै न कबहूं साहसी, दीन हीन को काज।
भूख्र सहै पै घास को, नाहिं भख्रै मृगराज।।

हीन जानि न विरोधिये, व तौ तन दुख्रदाये।
रजहू ठोकर मारिये, चढ़ै सीस पर आय।।

गुन सनेह-जुत होत हैं, ताही की छवि होत।
गुन-सनेह के दीप की, जैसे जोति उदोत।।

Brave is the offspring if parentage is brave,
A lioness produces only lions, not harts craven-faced.

Excessive goodness sometimes pain and suffering yields,
A parrot gets interned in cage, because his voice is sweet.

Everything is indued with its peculiar grace,
Food pacifies our hunger, water thirst allays.

A bouncing ball and a rolling coin much the same behave,
Now falling into your lap, now straying away.

Thieves take away the wealth which misers hoard with pain,
As honey stored by honey-bees, is by humans drained.

Charity should be given to those who really are in need,
As we give physic to those who suffer from some disease.

Approach even a lowly man to gather useful lore,
Even if it lies in dust, none rejects the gold.

*Soor vir ke bans mein, soor vir sut hoey,*
*Jeon sinhni ke garbh mein, hiran na upje koey.*

*Kahun kahun gun ten adhik, upjat dosh sareer,*
*Madhur baani boli ke, parat pinjara keer.*

*Apne apne samay par, sabko aadar hoey,*
*Bhojan pyaro bhook mein, tis mein payaro toey.*

*Dhan aru geind ju khel ko, dou ek subhaey,*
*Kar mein aawat chhinak mein, chhin mein kar ten jaaey.*

*Khaey na kharche soom dhan, chor sabe lejaaey,*
*Peechhe jeon madhumachhika, haath male pachhtaey.*

*Daan deen ko di lieye, mite darid ki peer,*
*Aushid wako dijieye, ja ke rog shareer.*

*Uttam vidya lijieye, Jadpi neech pe hoey,*
*Paryo apawan thaur ko, kanchan tajat na koey.*

सूर-बीर के बंस में, सूर-बीर सुत होय।
ज्यों सिंहिनि के गर्भ में, हिरन न उपजै कोय।।

कहूं कहूं गुन तें अधिक, उपजत दोष सरीर।
मधुर बानी बोलिकै, परत पींजरा कीर।।

अपने-अपने समय पर, सबकौ आदर होय।
भोजन प्यारो भूख्र में, तिस में प्यारो तोय।।

धन अरु गेंद जु, खेल कौ, दोऊ एक सुभाय।
कर में आवत छिनक में, छिन में कर तें जाय।।

खाय न खरचै सूम धन, चोर सबै ले जाय।
पीछे ज्यों मधुमच्छिका, हाथ मलै पछिताय।।

दान दीन को दीजिए, मिटै दरिद की पीर।
औषध वाको दीजिए, जाके रोग शरीर।।

उत्तम विद्या लीजिए, जदपि नीच पै होय।

A small mind cannot a big secret retain,
How can a half-litre can, one litre fluid contain?

Who will like to quit his sole safe resort,
A bird hovering round the boat, revolves round the mast.

He who is with wisdom blessed, lies beyond the reach of harm,
Rain cannot drench a man who is with an umbrella armed.

Union with one's beloved brings rare delight,
A peacock begins to strut and dance, seeing the clouds arrive.

One good son can enhance the family's wealth and pride,
As a single fragrant tree can perfume the garden wide.

The Supreme Being resides within, seek him no in distant wilds,
Like the deer seeking musk, which, in fact, within him lies.

Word by word one can peruse many a tome of learning wise,
As a traveller, step by step, can traverse miles and miles.

*Chhote nar ke pet mein, rahe na moti baat,*
*Aadh ser ke paatar mein, kaise ser samaat.*

*Ekai tha vishram ko, toko taji kanh jaaey.*
*Jeon panchhi sujahaz ko, uri uri tahan basaaey.*

*Jako budhi bal hot hai, tahi na ripu ko taraas,*
*Ghan boonden kah kari sake, sir par chhatna jaas.*

*Man bhawan ke milan se, sukh ko naahin chhor,*
*Boli uthe, nachi-nachi uthe, mor sunat ghangor.*

*Ek hi bhale saputra ten, sab kul bhalo kahaat,*
*Saras subasit bariksh tenh, jeon ban sakal basaat.*

*Chidanad ghat mein base, bujhat kahan niwas,*
*Jeon mrigmad mrig nabhi mein, dhoondat phirat suvaas.*

*Ek ek akshar parhe, jaane garanth vichar,*
*Paind-paindu chalat jo, pahunche kos hazaar.*

परयो अपावन ठौर को, कंचन तजत न कोय॥
छोटे नर के पेट में, रहे न मोटी बात।
आध सेर के पात्र में, कैसे सेर समात॥

एकै थल विश्राम को, ताको तजि कहं जाय।
ज्यों पंछी सुजहाज को, उड़ि उड़ि तहां बसाय॥

जाको बुद्धि-बल होत है, ताहि न रिपु को त्रास।
धन बूंदे कह करि सकें, सिर पर छतना जास॥

मन भावन के मिलन से, सुख्र को नाहिन छोर।
बोलि उठे नचि-नचि उठै, मोर सुनत घनघोर॥

एकहि भले सपुत्र तें, सब कुल भलो कहात।
सरस सुबासित बिरछ तें, ज्यों बन सकल बसात॥

चिदानंद घट में बसै, बूझत कहां निवास।
ज्यों मृगमद मृग नाभि में, ढूंढ़त फिरत सुवास॥

एक-एक अच्छर पढ़े, जाने ग्रंथ-विचार।
पेड-पैड़हू चलत जो, पहुँचे कोस हजार॥

Let your rival be incharge of your festive meets,
The more he spends the more it helps to boost your prestige.

Don't engage a weaker man in a fight or in debate,
If you win you earn no credit, if you lose, you lose your face.

It's true that people often do not practice what they preach,
One to show, one to use, the elephant has two sets of teeth.

None can alter or erase the cruel writ of fate,
The sea, though pater of the moon, cannot wash her scarred face.

The teacher can't give his best if his pupils show no worth,
A painter needs a canvas clean, ere he can ply his brush.

Always tap the right source which can serve your need,
A well at the mountain top cannot your thirst appease.

God's grace commensurates with your inward faith,
As a mirror reflects in truth the grace and foibles of your face.

*Ari ke kar mein dijieye, awsar ko adhikar,*
*Jeon jeon dravya lutaaey hai, teon teon jas bistaar.*

*Nibal jaani kijey nahin, kabhun ber, vivad,*
*Jeete kachhu sobha nahin, haare nindabaad.*

*Kahibo kachhu, karibo kachhu, hai jag ki vidhi dou,*
*Dekhan ke aur khaan ke, aur durd-rad hoey.*

*Kou door na karisake, vidhi ke ulte ank,*
*Udhadi pita tau chandrko, dhoey na sakeo kalank.*

*Guruhu sikhve gian gun, sishya subudhi jo hoey,*
*Likhe na khurdari bheet par, chitra chratera koey.*

*Kyon kijey aiso jatan, jate kaaj na hoey,*
*Parbat par khode kuaan, kaise nikre toey.*

*Dev sev phal det hai,ja ko jaiso bhaey,*
*Jaiso mukh par aarsi, dekho soi dikhaey.*

अरि के कर में दीजिए, अवसर को अधिकार।
ज्यों-ज्यों द्रव्य लुटाय है, त्यों-त्यों जस विस्तार।।

निबल जानि कीजै नहीं, कबहूं बैर विवाद।
जीते कछु सोभा नहीं, हारे निन्दावाद।।

कहिबो कछु करिवो कछु, है जग की विधि दोउ।
देखन के अरू खान के, और दुरद-रद होय।।

कोऊ दूर न करि सकै, विधि के उलटे अंक।
उदधि पिता तउ चंद्र को, धोय न सक्यो कलंक।।

गुरूहू सिखवै ज्ञान गुन, सिष्य सुबुद्धि जो होय।
लिखे न खुरदरि भीत पर, चित्र चितेरौ कोय।।

क्यों कीजे ऐसो जतन, जाते काज न होय।
परबत पर खोदै कुआं, कैसे निकरै तोय।।

देव सेव फल देत है, जाको जैसे भाय।
जैसो मुख पर आरसी, देखो सोई दिखाय।।

Give your ear to everyone, but do what serves your end,
You should aim at pleasing all, without giving offence.

The treasure-trove of knowledge holds a big surprise,
If you spend, it multiplies, if you hoard, it shrinks in size.

Remembering the Lord divine, drives a thousand ills away,
As a single spark of fire, can burn a whole heap of hay.

*Sunieye sab hi ki kahi, karieye sab-hit vichar,*
*Sab lok raji rahen, so kije upchaar.*

*Sarsuti ke bhandaar ki, bari apoorab baat,*
*Jeon jeon kharche, teon-teon barhe, bin kharche ghat jaat.*

*Japat ek hari naam ten, paatak koti bilaaey,*
*Ekhi kanika aagi ten, ghaas dher jari jaaey.*

सुनिये सब ही की कही, करिये सबहित-विचार।
सबलोक राजी रहैं, सो कीजे उपचार।

सरसुति के भंडार की, बड़ी अपूरब बात।।
ज्यो-ज्यों खरचे त्यों-त्यों बढ़े, बिन खरचे घटि जात।।

जपत इक हरिनाम तें, पातक कोटि बिलाय।
एकहि कनिका आगि तें, घास ढ़ेर जरि जाय।।

# Sheikh Farid

(1173–1266)

# Sheikh Farid (1173–1266)

Sheikh Farid is a highy honoured name among the saint-poets of India. He was born in 1173 at Khotwal, a small village in Multan district (now in Pakistan). After his preliminary education at home, he undertook a pilgrimage to Mecca at the age of sixteen. He then went to Kabul for education in Islamic faith and mystic lore. He is also said to visited Bukhara, Qandhar, Baghdad and Neeshapur, where he interacted with the sufi poets of the day. Returning to India he settled at Pak Patan. He sought instruction and inspiration from Khwaja Qutab-ul-din Bakhtiar, who was a devout follower of Khwaja Moin Din Chishti of Ajmer. After the death of his mentor he settled at Pak Patan along with his family. He became the father of a large family consisting of five sons and three daughters.

Farid was nurtured in a religious environment since his early days. This environment awakened and deepened his innate religious tendencies, and affected the colour and course of his poetry. But his religion was not the narrow wbigoted religion of one sect or creed. It was the religion of man, universally valid and beneficial. One of Farid's descendents, Sheikh Ibrahim, was a contemporary of Guru Nanak Dev, and it was through Sheikh Ibrahim that the *dohas* and *shabads* of Farid had entered into the text of *Guru Garanth Sahib*, the sacred scripture of the sikhs.

Besides being well-versed in Persian, Arabic and Punjabi, Farid was also conversant with Multani, Apbharansh and Prakrit, and he uses these languages judiciously in his poetry so as to make it widely accessible to all sorts of readers. Like his religion, the language and thought of his poetry was also catholic and all embracing. Even the illiterate people learn his verses by heart and ponder over them at leisure . By virtue of its elevating thought and delightful style, and because of its easy accesibility for an ordinary reader, his poetry has been for long a source of moral and spiritual stimulation, especially for the elderly generations in Punjab. A fore-runner of Kabir and Tulsi, his verse gives a foretaste of the spiritual and ethical flavour of the later poets.

Sheikh Farid died in 1266 at the age of 93.

# DOHAS OF SHEIKH FARID

Time canot be wished away however hard we try,
Every bride is married away when the time arrives.

The daughter leaves the parents' home, life from the body flies,
Who will hug the hollow frame,of life-force deprived?

She whom we long to see, hold in arms, hug her tight,
Disappears unannounced when the groom of death arrives.

A narrow bridge, hair-thin, spans across the river wide,
He who hears but does not heed, is swept away by the tide.

If your lips and heart concur, your love is deep and true,
Immature is your love if a gap divides the two.

To be a beggar at His door is a difficult task,
Where to throw off this bundle, which has become my albatross.

Even reason couldn't see the fire concealed in my heart,
Thanks to my Lord and luck, they saved me from the holocaust.

*Waqt na talta hai kabhi, koi ise samjhaey,*
*Waqt-e-muqarrar par dulhan, har ik beahi jaaey.*

*Maaeke se beti uthe, jism se jaan uth jaaey,*
*Khali qalib, jaan bin, kisko gale lagaey!*

*Ab tak sunte the jise aakar munh dikhlaaey,*
*Dulha malak-ul-maut ka jaan dulhan le jaaey.*

*Baal se bhi baareek pul darya paar karaaey,*
*Farida! Sun ke jo unsuni kare, so dhoka khaaey.*

*Dil se muhabbat jo karen, wahi aashiq sachche,*
*Zaahir-o-baatin mukhtalif, kahlawen kachche.*

*Darveshi us dar ki tau, bari hai mushkil baat,*
*Kahan yeh phainkoon potli, saath rahe din raat!*

*Dekh na paai aql bhi, chhupi hui woh aag,*
*Saaeen kaaran bach gaya, bhale the mere bhaag.*

वक़्त न टलता है कभी, कोई इसे समझाये।
वक्त-ए मुक़र्रर पर दुल्हन, हर इक ब्याही जाये।।

मैके से बेटी उठे, जिस्म से जान उठ जाये।
ख़ाली क़ालिब जान बिन, किस को गले लगाये।।

अब तक सुनते थे जिसे, आकर मुँह दिखलाये।
दूल्हा मलक-उल-मौत का, जान दुल्हन ले जाये।।

बाल से भी बारीक पुल, दरिया पार कराये।
फरीदा! सुन के जो अनसुनी करे, सो धोखा खाये।।

दिल से मुहब्बत जो करें, वही आशिक़ सच्चे।
ज़ाहिर-ओ-बातिन मुख़्तलिफ कहलावें कच्चे।।

दरवेशी उस दर की तो, बड़ी है मुश्किल बात।
कहां यह फेंकूँ पोटली, साथ रहे दिन रात।।

देख न पाई अक़्ल भी, छुपी हुई वो आग।
साईं कारण बच गया, भले थे मेरे भाग।।

Do not indulge in evil deeds, act like a sage,
Look within your heart, downward cast your gaze.

When someone hits you without a cause, do not seek revenge,
Kiss your enemy's feet, Fareeda, pursue your noble end.

When it was the time to reap, you were locked in slumber fast,
You have woken up too late when death on you his net has cast.

Cotton-white your beard has grown, high time to wake,
Birth is left far behind, death stands agape.

Ah! Those world-bewitching eyes which couldn't bear the collyrium touch,
I saw a row of carrion birds pecking at their lifeless flesh.

Greed and love can't co-exist, it is a ruse, a fraud,
How long can a broken shed bear the thunder blast?

Why scour the forest wild, or to the bed of thorns resort,
How can you find Him outside, He who lives inside your heart?

*Aqlmand hai tu agar, likh mat kaale lekh,*
*Sar neecha rakh kar sada, apne ander dekh.*

*Fareeda kuchh na kaho unhen, karen jo tum par waar,*
*Choomo unke paaon ko, pahuncho apne dwaar.*

*Jab khatna tha, mast tha, tujhe na tha kuchh yaad,*
*Fareeda! Pakki ho gai, maut ki ab bunyaad.*

*Kholo aankh Fareedji, daarhi hui kapaas,*
*Janam bahut peechhe raha, ant bahut hi paas.*

*Jin akhian jag moh liya, kaajal bhi tha bhaar,*
*Dekhi un par lagi hui, ik parind ki daar.*

*Lobh jahan wahan neih nahin, jhooti muhmial baat,*
*Toota chhappar kab talak, sah paaey barsaat!*

*Jungle jungle kya phire, kaanton par kya soey*
*Baahar kya dhoonde use, man ander jo hoey.*

अक़्लमंद है तू अगर, लिख मत काले लेख।
सर नीचा रख कर सदा, अपने अन्दर देख।।

फरीदा! कुछ न कहो उन्हें, करें जो तुम पर वार।
चूमो उनके पांव को, पहुँचो अपने द्वार।।

जब खटना था मस्त था, तुझे न था कुछ याद।
फरीदा! पक्की हो गई, मौत की अब बुनियाद।।

खोलो आंख फरीद जी, दाढ़ी हुई कपास।
जन्म बहुत पीछे रहा, अन्त बहुत ही पास।।

जिन अखियन जग मोह लिया, काजल भी था भार।
देखी उन पर लगी हुई, इक परिन्द की डार।।

लोभ जहां, वहां नेह नहीं, झूठी मुहमल बात।
टूटा छप्पर कब तलक, सह पाये बरसात।।

जंगल जंगल क्या फिरे, कांटों पर क्या सोये।
बाहर क्या ढूंढे उसे, मन अन्दर जो होये।।

Be content with plain bread and sips of water cool,
Do not feel tempted by the others' savoury foods.

Once I didn't feel tired though I ranged through hills and wilds,
But now to reach that cup at hand seems an arduous exercise.

Long and weary seems the night, difficult to pass,
Accursed are the lonely beings, condemned to wait and watch.

The street is full of muck and mire, with yearning deep is fired the heart,
If I walk I wet my blanket, if I stay I break my troth.

I didn't sleep with my husband, broken lie my limbs and bones,
Ask the poor widowed wife, how she spends her life alone!

Vain to hope for luscious grape, when brambly bush is what you sow,
It is to dream of silken robes, while spinning cotton coarse.

Why complain that youth will die, love for the Lord should remain alive,
Many a youth, deprived of love, has withered away and died.

*Rookhi sookhi khaaey ke thanda paani pi,*
*Dekh parai chopri mat tarsaaeyeji*

*Jungle parbat phir ke bhi, thak kar hua na choor,*
*Aaj yeh kooza lag raha, jaise koson door.*

*Raaten mushkil se katen, lambi aur udaas,*
*Laanat unki zindagi, jinhen paraai aas.*

*Gali mein keechar, door ghar, saath peea ke neh,*
*Chaloon tau bheege kambli, rahoon tau toote neh.*

*Aaj na soi kant sang, ang ang toota jaaey,*
*Poochh duhagan se zara, Kaise umar bitaey.*

*Kikar bo kar dil mein, hai angooron ki taak,*
*Kaaten oon aur khwab mein, resham ki poshaak.*

*Joban jaate kyon daroon, peaa sang preet na jaaey,*
*Kitne joban preet bin, sookh gaye kumlhaaey.*

रूखी सूखी खाय के ठँडा पानी पी।
देख पराई चोपड़ी मत तरसाइये जी।।

जंगल परबत फिर के भी, थक कर हुआ न चूर,।
आज यह कूज़ा लग रहा, जैसे कोसों दूर।।

रातें मुश्किल से कटें, लम्बी और उदास।
लानत उनकी ज़िन्दगी, जिन्हें पराई आस।।

गली में कीचड़, दूर घर, साथ पिया के नेह।
चलूं तो भीगे कम्बली, रहूं तो टूटे नेह।।

आज न सोई कंत संग, अंग अंग टूटा जाये।
पूछ दुहागन से ज़रा, केसे उम्र बिताये।।

कीकर बोकर दिल में है, अंगूरो की ताक।
कातें ऊन और ख़्वाब में, रेशम की पोशाक।।

जोबन जाते क्यूं डरूं, पिय संग प्रीत न जाये।
कितने जोबन प्रीत बिन, सूख गये कुम्हलाये।।

Everyone complains of parting, parting is the king and lord,
He who hasn't felt the pangs is a barren burial yard.

For half your life you groped your way, the rest half you slept away,
What for were you sent on earth, God will ask you one day.

Age has caught up with you, Farid, web-like shakes your body frail,
Even if allowed a hundred years, dust will be your final fate.

This house overflows wtih flavour that hasn't got a grain to show,
He shall punish or compensate, the Lord God who all doth know.

Even the kings once heralded by drums, pipes and bards,
Were one day rendered helpless, done to dust at last.

Right in front of the two lamps, the herald of death stood entrenched,
Ravaged the fort, robbed my life, extinguished both the lamps.

Serve thou the Lord supreme, all doubts dissolve,
Patient like the trees should be the mendicants of God.

*Birha birha sab kah rahe, birah tau hai sultan,*
*Jis mein birah paida na ho, woh tan hai shamshan.*

*Chaar ganwaaey bhatkte, so ke ganwaaey chaar,*
*Rub maange lekha ki tu aaya tha kis kaar.*

*Boorhe hue Farid ji, kaaney deih ka jaal,*
*Ant tau hoga khaak mein, chaahe milen sau saal.*

*Ik ghar mein aata bahut, ik mein na namak samaan,*
*Maar pare aage kise, tab hogi pahchaan.*

*Chhatar, damamey, tootiaan, bhaat the jin ki jaan,*
*Farida, woh bhi yatim ban, ja soey shamshan.*

*Donon deon ke saamne, malak-ul-maut khara,*
*Garh jeeta, ghat loot kar, chal diya dieye bujha.*

*Sahib ki kar chaakri, dil se bharm mita,*
*Darveshon ko chahiye, dheeraj, peron sa.*

बिरह बिरह सब कह रहे, बिरह तो है सुलतान।
जिस में बिरह पैदा न हो, वो तन है शमशान।।

चार गंवाये भटकते, सो के गंवाये चार।
रब मांगे लेखा कि तू, आया था किस कार।।

बूढ़े हुए फरीद जी, कांपे देह का जाल।
अन्त तो होगा ख़ाक में, चाहे मिलें सौ साल।।

इक घर में आटा बहुत, इक में न नमक समान।
मार पड़े आगे किसे, तब होगी पहचान।।

छत्र, दमामे, तूतियां, भाट थे जिनकी जान।
फरीदा! वो भी यतीम बन, जा सोये शमशान।।

दोनों दियों के सामने, मलक-उल-मौत खड़ा।
गढ़ जीता, घट लूट कर, चल दिया दिये बुझा।।

साहिब की कर चाकरी, दिल से भरम मिटा।
दरवेशों को चाहिए, धीरज पेड़ों सा।।

Not a drop of blood doth flow if someone cuts his body in twain,
Bloodless is his body who is dyed in God's name.

Cotton-white your beard and moustache, cotton like your locks,
High time, O sluggard, to abandon the sensual path.

When unmarried, I longed for marriage, now married, I rue my fate,
I'm worried day and night, I can't regain my virgin state.

All the water birds have flown which once enlivened this lake,
The lake too will dry up, and the lotuses hang dismayed.

In the worm-infested earth, on a hard brick pillowed,
The body sleeps for centuries in the same static pose.

He who doesn't offer prayers five times a day,
Doesn't visit the mosque for worship, attains the dog's state.

Wake up Farid, perform ablution, morning prayers attend,
Cut off your worthless head, if it doesn't bend.

*Boond na nikle khoon ki, jo tan cheere koey,*
*Rab ke rang mein jo ranga, us tan lahu na hoey.*

*Sar kapaas, daarhi kapaas, moonchh bhi hui kapaas,*
*Re man ghafil banwre, chhore na kyon rang raas!*

*Jab thi kunwari, chaav the, beaahi tau janjaal,*
*Phir na kunwari ban sakoon, khaawe yehi khyaal.*

*Chale gaye panchhi woh sab, jin se basa tha taal,*
*Sookhega yeh taal bhi, honge kanwal behaal.*

*Keeron bhari zameen mein, eent sirhaane hoey,*
*Yugon yugon tak jism tab, ek hi karwat soey.*

*Paanchon waqt namaz ko, masjid mein jo na aaey,*
*Kare na jo bhi bandagi, sag ka darja paaey.*

*Utho Farid, Wuzu karo, subah ki parho namaz,*
*Kare na sijda, kaat do apna sar-e-na saaz.*

बून्द न निकले ख़ून की, जो तन चीरे कोय।
रब के रंग में जो रंगा, उस तन लहू न होय।।

सिर कपास दाढ़ी कपास, मूछ भी हुई कपास।
रे मन ग़ाफ़िल बावरे, छोड़े न क्यों रंग रास।।

जब थी कुंवारी चाव थे, ब्याही तो जंजाल।
फिर न कुंवारी बन सकूं, ख्रावे यही ख़याल।।

चले गये पंछी वो सब, जिनमें बसा था ताल।
सूखेगा यह ताल भी, होंगे कंवल बेहाल।।

कीड़ो भरी ज़मीन में, ईंट सिरहाने होय।
युगों युगों तक जिस्म तब, एक ही करवट सोये।।

पांचों वक़्त नमाज़ को, मस्जिद में जो न आये।
करे न जो भी बन्दगी, सग का दर्जा पाये।।

उठो फरीद वूज़ू करो, सुबह की पढ़ो नमाज़।
करे न सजदा, काट दो, अपना सर-ए-नासाज़।।

The head that doesn't bend in prayer, should be punished hard,
Burn it as the firewood to boil the cooking pot.

Where are your parents now who gave you birth and life?
They have gone, quitting you, still you don't realize!

Level down your mind, Farid, doubt and fear dispel,
You cannot then be daunted by the flashing fires of hell.

We are the visitor birds, the world a beauteous grove,
The morning drum has sounded, pack your goods and go!

No dearth of pleasant talkers here, but a man of worth is rare,
I am smouldering like the dung-cake, but find a lover nowhere.

I wish you had cut off my head, when you had cut my navel chord,
It could then have saved me from the life's tormenting task.

Eyes, teeth and legs have gone, ears have grown deaf,
With the slackening of the body, all the dear ones have left.

*Saijde mein na jo sar jhuke, do use yehi saza,*
*Haandi tale jalaey ke, kaam lo eendhan ka.*

*Kahan tire maan baap hain, jinhon ne janam diya,*
*Chhor ke tujhko chal dieye, phir bhi na tu samjha.*

*Fareeda man humwaar kar, wahm-o-gumaan ko tayaag,*
*Aage kabhi na aaegi, dozakh ki koi aag.*

*Duniya suhana bagh hai, hum panchhi mehmaan,*
*Baji hai naubat subah ki, baandho ab samaan.*

*Baaton ke dhani beeseon,asl mile nahin ek,*
*Sulgoon uple ki tarah,mile na saajan nek.*

*Kyon na gala kata gira, kaati thi jab naal,*
*Sahne na parte itne dukh, aur itne janjaal.*

*Daant, aankhen, taangen gaiein, kaan hue bahre,*
*Jism dhala kya sab aziz us ko chhor gaye.*

सजदे में न जो सर झुके, दो उसे यही सज़ा।
हांडी तले जलाय के, काम लो ईंधन का।।

कहां तिरे मां-बाप हैं, जिन्होंने जन्म दिया।
छोड़ के तुझको चल दिये, फिर भी न तू समझा।।

फरीदा! मन हमवार कर, वहम-ओ गुमां को त्याग।
आगे कभी न आएगी, दोज़ख़ की कोई आग।।

दुनिया सुहाना बाग़ है, हम पंछी मेहमान।
बजी है नौबत सुबह की, बांधो अब सामान।।

बातों के धनी बीसियों, अस्ल मिले नहीं एक।
सुलगूं उपले की तरह, मिले न साजन नेक।।

क्यूं न गला कट गिरा, काटी थी जब नाल।
सहने न पड़ते इतने दुख, और इतने जंजाल।।

दाँत, आँखें, टाँगें गईं, कान हुए बहरे।
जिस्म ढ़ला क्या सब अज़ीज, उसको छोड़ गये।।

The night is scattering camphor, they miss the scent who sleep,
Even they will lose their share, who are half-asleep.

Am I the only sorrow-stung? Common are the sad strains,
I see a fire wide-spread, when I watch from a higher plane.

Do not erode your banks, river, you'll have to answer for,
Agreed that your ebb and flow is controlled by the will of God.

Do good even to the bad, renounce revenge and wrath,
This will ensure good health for you, nothing will it cost.

Bodily needs multiply, with them increase the ills of life,
Plug your ears with cotton wool, admit no voice deep inside.

The streams of honey flow in heaven, God's dates are ripe,
But you can't enjoy this feast unless you quit this life.

The body has become a skeleton dry, the crows at the soles peck,
Still one cannot meet God, see the man's luck!

*Raat mein kastoori bante, bhag mile nahin soey,*
*Adhjaga bhi neend mein, apna hissa khoey.*

*Main samjhoon dukh bas mujhe, sakal jagat dukh raag,*
*Dekhoon ooncha ho ke tau, ghar ghar yehi hai aag.*

*Nadii na apna tat gira, dena parega hisaab,*
*Mana, rab ki raza mein hain tere pech-o-taab.*

*Bure ka bhi kijieye bhala, man mein na gussa aaey,*
*Deih rogon se bachi rahe, pass se kuchh bhi na jaaey.*

*Tan ki maangen barh rahin, aur dukh barhta jaaey,*
*Kaanon mein bhar li rooi, kuchh bhi na ander aaey.*

*Rab ki khajooren hain paki, shahd ki nadi bahe,*
*Umr se manfi ho ke hi, din ras mein guzre.*

*Tan sookha, pinjar hua, talwe nochen kaag,*
*Ab bhi na rab pahunche, tau phir bande ka bhaag.*

रात में कस्तूरी बंटे, भाग मिले नहीं सोये।
अधजागा भी नींद में, अपना हिस्सा खोये।।

मैं समझूं दुख बस मुझे, सकल जगत दुख-राग।
देखूं ऊँचा हो के तो, घर घर यही है आग।।

नदी! न अपना तट गिरा, देना पड़ेगा हिसाब।
माना, रब की रज़ा में है, तेरे पेच-ओ ताब।।

बुरे का भी कीजै भला, मन में न गुस्सा आये।
देह रोगों से बची रहे, पास से कुछ भी न जाये।।

तन की मांगें बढ़ रहीं, और दुख बढ़ता जाये।
कानों में भर ली रूई, कुछ भी न अन्दर आये।।

रब की खजूरें हैं पकी, शहद की नदी बहे।
उम्र से मन्फ़ी हो के ही, दिन रस में गुज़रे।।

तन सूखा, पिंजर हुआ, तलुवे नोचें काग।
अब भी न रब पहुँचे तो फिर, बन्दे का है भाग।।

Nibble away my skeleton, crow, eat the flesh from every part,
But pray, spare my eyes with which I hope to see my Lord.

Do not nibble at my body, be kind, O crow, depart,
Do not eat my tabernacle wherein my Lord resorts.

"Come back home, you homeless man", thus calls the grave,
"I am your destined goal, do not be afraid."

I have seen many a man before my eyes depart,
Why shouldn't I guard my interest, when everyman is self-engrossed.

Who can console the tree on the river bank inlaid,
How long can a pot of clay hold against the surging spate?

The shore of death looks like a river bank unveiled,
The flaming hell lies beyond, uproarious with wails.

Some people understand it all, some the signs ignore,
Your deeds alone will support your case, nothing else avails.

*Kaga! pinjar noch kar, khalo sara maas,*
*Mat chhoona yeh do nain, peaa dekhan ki aas.*

*Kaga! noch na yeh badan, bas mein hai tau ur ja,*
*Jis mein mera saain base, uska maas na kha.*

*Qabar sada yeh de rahi, beghar, ghar ko aa,*
*Main hi hoon manzil tiri, mujh se mat ghabra.*

*Kitne hi mere dekhte, chhor gaye hain praan,*
*Sabko jab apni pari, rakhoon apna dhayaan.*

*Nadi kinare per ka dheeraj kaun bandhaey,*
*Kachcha bartan kab talak paani ko rakh paaey.*

*Lage kinara maut ka, jon darya ka chhor,*
*Aage tapte narak mein, hahakaar ka shor.*

*Kuchh samajhen sab aur kuchh phirte beparwah,*
*Karm jo duniya mein kieye, bante wahi gawah.*

कागा! पिंजर नोच कर, खालो सारा मास।
मत छुइयो यह दो नयन, पिय देखन की आस।।

कागा! नोच न यह बदन, बस में है तो उड़ जा।
जिस में मिरा साईं बसे, उसका मास न खा।।

क़ब्र सदा यह दे रही, बेघर घर को आ।
मैं ही हूं मंज़िल तिरी, मुझसे मत घबरा।।

कितने ही मेरे देखते, छोड़ गये हैं प्राण।
सबको जब अपनी पड़ी, रक्खूं अपना ध्यान।।

नदी किनारे पेड़ का, धीरज कौन बंधाय।
कच्चा बर्तन कब तलक, पानी को रख पाय।।

लगे किनारा मौत का, ज्यूं दरिया का छोर।
आगे तपते नर्क में, हाहाकार का शोर।।

कुछ समझें सब और कुछ, फिरते बेपरवाह।
कर्म जो दुनिया में किये, बनते वही गवाह।।

Frolicking by the river-side, a stork was playing with straws,
Suddenly swooped an eagle on the playful stork.

With a sudden strike, God's falcon undid the life's task,
The sudden blow resulted in what never was dreamt or thought.

Food and water are necessary to sustain our breath and being,
Man comes to his world with many a pleasant dream.

When the god of death arrives, breaking walls and doors,
The dear ones prepare the body, in coffin sheets adorn.

Four shoulders carry the corpse to the burial yard,
The deeds a man has done in life, help him cross he bar.

Hats off to the birds who in desert wilds resort,
Roll on sand, peck on stones, yet never forget to thank their Lord.

Season has changed, the forest shivers, autumn sings supreme,
Nothing has escaped the change, all over I have seen.

*Nadi kinare baith ke bagula khel kare,*
*Khel rahe us hans par yakdam baaz pare.*

*Baaz pare us rab ke jo, sab kuchh chhoot gaya,*
*Jo na tha man chit dhayaar mein, rab ne woh kaam kiya.*

*Paani ann se hi chalen bhaari deih ke shawaas,*
*Banda jag mein aaey hai, le ke suhani aas.*

*Aaey malak-ul-maut jab, tor ke sab dwaar,*
*Bhai bandhu baandh kar, karen use tayyaar.*

*Chala hai banda chaar ke, kaandhon par aswaar,*
*Kaam jo is jag mein kieye, kaam aaein us paar.*

*Dasht mein base parind jo, un par main qurbaan,*
*Thal mein rahen, kankar chunden, rab ka na chhoren dhayaan.*

*Rut badli, ban kaanp utha, patjhar ka hai zor,*
*Kuchh bhi na paainda mila, dhoonde chaaron aur.*

नदी किनारे बैठ के, बगुला खोल करे।
खोल रहे उस हंस पर, यकदम बाज़ पड़े।।

बाज़ पड़े उस रब के जो, सब कुछ छूट गया।
जो न था मन चित्त ध्यान में, रब ने वो काम किया।।

पानी अन्न से ही चले, भारी देह के श्वास।
बंदा जग में आये है, ले के सुहानी आस।।

आये मलक-उल-मौत जब, तोड़ के सारे द्वार।
भाई बन्धू बांध कर, करें उसे तैयार।।

चला है बन्दा चार के, कांधों पर असवार।
कर्म जो इस जग में किये, काम आयें उस पार।।

दश्त में बसे परिन्द जो, उन पर मैं कुर्बान।
थल में रहें कंकर-चुगें, रब का न छोड़े ध्यान।।

रुत बदली, बन कांप उठा, पतझड़ का है ज़ोर।
कुछ भी न पाईन्दः मिला, ढूंढे चारों ओर।।

I shudder to think of those who do not think of God,
Both here and hereafter, they'll rue their lot.

You lived your life like the dead, till the end you didn't wake,
You have forgotten God, thee He didn't forsake.

If you have the bow of patience, with the string of patience taut,
On top an arrow, patience-steeled, God will help your cause.

Mendicancy is a difficult task, on top,your love is skin-deep,
Not many men in this field did really succeed.

God lives in every heart, be not curt or cruel,
Do not break any heart, each one is a precious jewel.

Those dyed in God's love, achieve the vision blest,
Those who forget Him, are a burden on this earth

You are my guardian, Lord, pray pardon my faults,
Grant me your devotion, this is what I ask.

*Dekh he unko dar lage, bhool gaye jo naam,*
*Dheron dukh paaen yahaan, aage na koi maqaam.*

*Zinda mooey samaan tu, jaga na aakhir-e-shab,*
*Tu bhoola rab ko magar, bhoola tujhe na rab.*

*Sabr ki man mein kamaan ho, sabr ki hi ho dore,*
*Sabar ka hi jab tir ho, khaaliq teri aur.*

*Darveshi mushkil bari, satahi teri pareet,*
*Hain kitne jin se chali, darveshi ki reet.*

*Sab mein wahi maalik basa, pheeke bol na bol,*
*Dil na kisi ka tor tu, sab moti anmol.*

*Range Khuda ke ishq mein, mile unhen deedaar,*
*Bhoole uska naam jo, bane zameen par bhaar.*

*Teri panah mein hoon Khuda, bakhsheo meri zaat,*
*Sheikh Farid ko bandagi, ki deejo khairaat.*

देख़ के उनको डर लगे, भूल गये जो नाम।
ढेरों दुख़ पायें यहां, आगे न कोई मक़ाम।।

ज़िन्दा मुए समान तू, जगा न आख़िर-ए-शब।
तू भूला रब को मगर, भूला तुझे न रब।।

सब्र की मन में कमान हो, सब्र की ही हो डोर।
सब्र का ही जब तीर हो, ख़ालिक़ तेरी ओर।।

दरवेशी मुश्किल बड़ी, सतही तेरी प्रीत।
हैं कितने जिनसे चली, दरवेशी की रीत।।

सब में वही मालिक बसा, फीके बोल न बोल।
दिल न किसी का तोड़ तू, सब मोती अनमोल।।

रंगे ख़ुदा के इश्क में, मिले उन्हें दीदार।
भूले उनका नाम जो, बने ज़मी पर भार।।

तेरी पनाह में हूं ख़ुदा, बख़्शियो मेरी ज़ात।
शेख़ फ़रीद को बन्दगी, की दीजो ख़ैरात।।

He who is childlike in spite of being wise,
Thinks he is a victor, though vanquished in the fight,

In spite of being poor, gives with a generous hand,
Such a man, remember, is a real acolyte.

Attune your mind with God, Farid ji thus spake,
This body will turn to dust, when buried in the grave.

The union eve has arrived, tempting are the passions bold,
But when in the indulgent mood, keep your mind controlled.

No one has lived, nor will live forever on this earth,
Many a man before you has sat on your berth.

Lightning-like is Sawan month, Chetar burns, Kartik stings,
But with your love by your side, even winter seems spring.

"What has given you, koel, coal-black complexion"?
I have been burnt black by the fire of separation.

How can one be happy in the absence of one's mate,
May the gracious God our meeting facilitate!

*Aaqil ho kar tifle hai, shakt hai lage ashakt,*
*Pass nahin kuchh phir bhi de, vahi hai sachcha bhagat.*

*Bole Sheikh Farid ji, rab se joro dhayaan,*
*Yeh tan qabar mein ja ke tau, hoga khaak samaan.*

*Wasal ki Sheikh Farid ji, aai aaj ki shaam,*
*Man ko lubhate nafas ki, bas mein rahe lagaam.*

*Jag mein hamesha ke lieye, ruka na koi ruke,*
*Jis aasan baithe hain hum, kitne baith chuke.*

*Sawan bijli, Chet aag, kartik milen kalang,*
*Sardi mein achha lage, peea ho jab ang sang.*

*Kaise hui tu koel kaali,*
*Peaa bin hui main jaljal kaali.*

*Peaa bin kaise sukh paaey,*
*Kripa kare, prabhu aap milaaey.*

आक़िल हो कर तिफ़्ल है, शक्त है लगे अशक्त।
पास नहीं कुछ फिर भी दे, वही है सच्चा भक्त।।

बोले शेख़ फ़रीद जी, रब से जोड़ो ध्यान।
यह तन कब्र में जा के तो, होगा ख़ाक समान।।

वस्ल की शेख़ फरीद जी, आई आज की शाम।
मन को लुभाते नफ़स की, बस में रहे लगाम।।

जग में हमेशा के लिए, रुका न कोई रुके।
जिस आसन बैठे हैं हम, कितने बैठ चुके।।

सावन बिजली, चेत आग, कत्तक मिलें कलंग।
सर्दी में अच्छा लगे, पिया हो जब अंग संग।।

कैसे हुई तू कोयल काली।
पिया बिन हुई मैं जल जल काली।।

पिया बिना कैसे सुख पाये।
कृपा करे प्रभू आप मिलाये।।

Dreadful dark is the well, all alone I stand,
Without a friend or comrade, none to hold my hand.

By God'grace I became a member of a saintly meet,
Which helped me meet my Lord, my sole anchor-sheet.

The way is dark and difficult, narrow is the road,
Narrower than even the edge of a sword,

Walking over which your breath you have to hold,
Sheikh Farid, take care of your weakling fold.

What words, what magic verse, what virtues to adopt,
What clothes to wear to win over my Lord.

Humble speech, patient mind, a loud, persistent call,
Equipped with these accoutrements, you can win your lord.

When the Lord gives the call, Farid says, O mates,
The body crumbling down like clay, deep obeisance pays.

*Kuaan bhayankar, aur main akeli,*
*Koi na saathi, koi na beli.*

*Prabhu kripa sat sangat le li,*
*Mila mujhe mira allah beli.*

*Rah dukh bhari aur taareek,*
*Tegh ki dhaar se bhi baareek,*

*Us par chalna bahut mahaal,*
*Sheikh Fareedi, panth sambhaal.*

*Shabad kaun sa, kaun gun, mantar kaun anant,*
*Pahnoon kaun libaas main, bas mein howe kant.*

*Shabad naman aur sabr gun, waani naad anant,*
*In teenon ko orh le, bas mein howe kant.*

*Kahe Farid saheleo! Jab saain bulaaey,*
*Hans anmna chale, jism mitti ho jaaey.*

कुआं भयंकर और मैं अकेली।
कोई न साथी कोई न बेली।।

प्रभू कृपा सत संगत ले ली।
मिला मुझे मिरा अल्लाह बेली।।

राह दुख्ख भरी और तारीक।
तेग की धार से भी बारीक।।

उस पर चलना बहुत मुहाल।
शेख़ फ़रीदा! पंथ संभाल।।

शब्द कौन सा, कौन गुण, मंतर कौन अनन्त।
पहनूं कौन लिबास मैं, बस में होवे कंत।।

शब्द नमन और सब्र गुण, वाणी नाद अनन्त।
इन तीनों को ओढ़ ले, बस में होवे कंत।।

कहे फ़रीद सहेलियो! जब साईं बुलाये।
हंस अनमना चले, जिस्म मिट्टी हो जाय।।

Sugar-coated poison plants on every side stand,
Ah, the wretched! What they sowed, their crops corrupt the land.

Let the body burn like furnace, fuel-like the bones blaze,
If the feet are tired, I'll walk on head to see my Lord's face.

Don't talk ill of dust, it's a thing which has no like,
It lies beneath when we are alive, wraps us up when we die.

A lonely bird in the lake, by a hundred hunters chased,
The body trapped in the waves, God alone can save.

Sweet-tongued, saintly-shaped, but fraudulent at heart,
Bright and white exterior, inside is deadly dark.

Be thou, Farida, the pathway grass, if you hope to meet your lord,
It's trampled over by one and all, except the few who arrive last.

The colourful pot has gone aburst, broken lies the thread of breath,
He'll now turn to another house, Azazel, the herald of death.

*Vish ke paude har taraf, lep khaand ka orh,*
*Mare beejte aur kuchh, beeji bhi gaye chhor.*

*Jism tape tandoor sa, haad bane eendhan,*
*Paaon thaken, chaloon sar ke bal, jo ho peaa milan.*

*Khaak ki ninda mat karo, is sa aur na koey,*
*Jeete ji patron tale, maren tau oopar hoey.*

*Panchhi tanha taal mein, aur sayyaad pachaas.*
*Tan lahron mein phans gaya, Saain!, teri aas!*

*Bhes faqiri, munh mein gur, dil mein magar hai ghaat,*
*Baahar sab ujla lage, ander kaali raat.*

*Farida! ban raste ki ghaas, agar hai peaa milan ki aas,*
*Raunden sab bach paaen kuchh ek, jo pahunchen saain ke dar nek.*

*Phoot gaya rangeen ghara, tooti saans ki dor,*
*Azazel ab chal para, agle ghar ki aur.*

विष के पौदे हर तरफ़, लेप खांड की ओढ़।
मरे बीजते और कुछ, बीजी भी गये छोड़।।

जिस्म तपे तन्दूर सा, हाड़ बने ईंधन।
पांव थके चलूं सर के बल, जो हो पिया मिलन।।

ख़ाक की निन्दा मत करो, इस सा और न कोय।
जीते जी पैरों तले, मरें तो ऊपर होय।।

पंछी तन्हा ताल में, और सय्याद पचास।
तन लहरों में फंस गया, साईं! तेरी आस।।

भेस फ़क़ीरी, मुंह में गुड़, दिल में मगर है घात।
बाहर सब उजला लगे, अन्दर काली रात।।

फ़रीदा! बन रस्ते की घास, अगर है पिया मिलन की आस।
रुंदें सब बच पायें कुछ एक, जो पहुंचे साईं के दर नेक।।

फूट गया रंगीन घड़ा, टूटी सांस की डोर।
अज़ाज़ील अब चल पड़ा, अगले घर की ओर।।

Look for a limpid lake, if you want to quench your thirst,
What use finding a pond full of dirt and slush?

Water can't revive the crop, singed by flood,
A God-abandoned widow will weep tears of blood.

Reform yourself and merge in me, see the dawn of hope,
The entire world will hug you close, surrender at my feet.

The palaces too are getting deserted, haunted seems the barren waste,
The souls are taking charge of their new alloted graves.

Meditate on God, Sheikh, The world, is a transient place.

I wring my hands, roll in grief,
Searching thee, I have lost my peace,

You, O lord, are annoyed with me,
The fault is mine, not of thee.

I didn't realize your worth in time,
Too late it is to regret and pine.

*Vahi sarovar dhoond tu, jaha bane kuch baat,*
*Chhappar dhoonde kya mile, kichad aave haath.*

*Jal se jali kheti, jal main hari na hoye,*
*Rab ki duhagan umra bhar, khoon ke aansoo roye.*

*Sanvre tau mujh main meele, sukh ka savera hoye,*
*Jau tu mera ho rahe, sab jag tera hoye.*

*Mahal bhi soone ho rahe, basa jaami ka tal,*
*Roohen kaabij rahin, kabron pe har pal.*
*Karo bandagi shaikh jee, rukshat aaj ki kal.*

*Haath maloo dukh dariya doobe,*
*Huyee baavari, saai dhoondoo.*

*Saai! tere man main rosh,*
*Main daushi, nahi tera daush.*

*Tu Malak, tiri qadar na jaani,*
*Joban khoya, tab pahchani.*

वही सरोवर ढूंढ तू, जहां बने कुछ बात।
छप्पर ढूंढे क्या मिले, कीचड़ आवे हाथ॥

जल से जली खेती कभी, जल में हरी न होये।
रब की दुहागन उम्र भर, ख़ून के आंसू रोये॥

संवरे तो मुझ में मिले, सुख का सवेरा होय।
जो तू मेरा ही रहे, सब जग तेरा होय॥

महल भी सूने हो रहे, बसा ज़मीं का तल।
रुहें काबिज़ रहीं, क़ब्रों पे हर पल।
करो बन्दगी शेख़ जी, रुख़सत आज कि कल॥

हाथ मलूं दुख दरिया डूबूं।
हुई बावरी, साईं ढूंढूं॥

साईं! तेरे मन में रोष।
मैं दोषी, नहीं तेरा दोष॥

तू मालिक, तिरी क़द्र न जानी।
जोबन खोया, तब पहचानी॥

You are worrying about the turban, lest it gets spoiled,
The sluggard soul knows not the head is also getting wired.

Sugar, jaggery, honey milk, all, no doubt are sweet,
But not as sweet as my Lord, who is a rare treat

You are married just in name, if neglected by your lord,
Not a night you spend in peace, in parent's house, or husband's lodge.

Let my blanket get drenched, and heaven send torrential rain,
Despite all, I'll visit my Lord, lest my love is brought to shame,

It is hard to fight passion, despite stern advise,
Reprimand eats no ice, when the mind is deep inclined.

When the strong climb the heights, the weak feel inspired,
Minds mired in greed, are always torn and tired.

If sesame seeds are small in quantity, do not stretch your grasp,
If the Lord is like child-like small, bend while you talk.

*Pagdi ka hee dhyan hai, mailee na hone paye,*
*Gaaphil rooha kau kya khabar, sar ko bhi mitti khaye.*

*Shakkar, khaand aur shahad, good, doodh bhaisn ka hoye,*
*Yeh sab meethe hain magar, raab se na meetha koye.*

*Rahe suhagaan naam ki, peeya jo na pooche baat,*
*Maika ya sasuraal ho, kate na ek bhi raat.*

*Chahe bheege kambli, rab barsaye maih,*
*Jaye miloon saajan se main, toote kahin na naih.*

*Rauj naseehat dijiye, phir na phir bhi dhyaan,*
*Oonche bol bhi beassar, man main ho jab shaitaan.*

*Paar karei balvan jab, nirbal paanve bal,*
*Dhan daulat laalchi, dookh paanve har pal.*

*Fareeda! til kam hao agar, sambhal ke bhariye haath,*
*Saai bal saman ho, jhook kar keeje baat.*

पगड़ी का ही ध्यान है, मैली न होने पाये।
ग़ाफ़िल रूह को क्या ख़बर, सर को भी मिट्टी खाये।।

शक्कर, खांड और शहद, गुड़, दूध भैंस का होय।
यह सब मीठे हैं मगर, रब से न मीठा कोय।।

रहे सुहागन नाम की, पिया जो न पूछे बात।
मैका या ससुराल हो, कटे न इक भी रात।।

चाहे भीगे कम्बली, रब बरसाये मेह।
जाय मिलूं साजन से मैं, टूटे कहीं न नेह।।

रोज़ नसीहत दीजिए, फिर न फिर भी ध्यान।
ऊंचे बोल भी बेअसर, मन में हो जब शैतान।।

पार करें बलवान जब, निर्बल पांवें बल।
धन दौलत लालची, दुख पांवे हर पल।।

फरीदा! तिल कम हों अगर, संभल के भरिये हाथ।
साईं बाल समान हो, झुक कर कीजै बात।।

| | | |
|---|---|---|
| 16. | How to Succeed in Life | 125/- |
| 17. | How to Reduce Tension | 125/- |
| 18. | A Book of Stenography | 95/- |
| 19. | Business Letters | 90/- |
| 20. | Baby Names for Boys | 75/- |
| 21. | Baby Names for Girls | 75/- |
| 22. | Non Vegetarian Delights | 95/- |
| 23. | Pure Vegetarian Delights | 95/- |
| 24. | Indian National Congress | 450/- |
| 25. | Jokes for All | 75/- |

**(Publishers & Distributors)**
4263/3, Ansari Road, Daryaganj, New Delhi - 110002
Phone.: 32903912, 23280047, 9811594448
E-mail: lotus_press@sify.com
Website: www.lotuspress.co.in